P9-DYJ-862

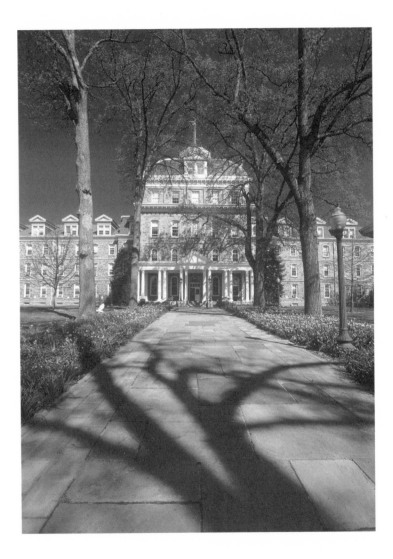

The publication of *The Meaning of Swarthmore* was made possible by a grant from Mark R. Pattis '75 and The Pattis Family Foundation, Highland Park, Illinois.

Copyright © 2004 by Swarthmore College
500 College Avenue
Swarthmore PA 19081-1390

All rights reserved.

No part of this publication may be reproduced, stored in a retrieval system, or transmitted in any form or by any means, electronic, mechanical, photocopying, recording, or otherwise, without prior permission, in writing, of Swarthmore College. Authorization to photocopy items for internal or personal use of specific clients is granted by the copyright owner.

ISBN 0-9748293-0-7

Dustjacket and book design by Suzanne DeMott Gaadt, Gaadt Perspectives LLC
Front cover photograph by Bob Krist; back cover photograph by Terry Wild
Photographs are from the collection of the Friends Historical Library of Swarthmore College. The publisher gratefully acknowledges the work of the following photographers: Henry Grant Compton, Peter Dechert, Steven Goldblatt '67, Walter Holt, Bob Krist, Eleftherios Kostans, Philip Mayer, Martin Natvig, David Sahagian, Steve Schapiro, James Tracy, and Lawrence Williams.

Printed in the United States of America

The
Meaning of
Swarthmore

Edited by
Roger Youman '53

Foreword by
President Alfred H. Bloom

SWARTHMORE

Contents

Foreword

Alfred H. Bloom
President of Swarthmore College

I am delighted to present this collection of essays offered by Swarthmore alumni about this extraordinary institution. Reflecting the independence of mind and sensibility nourished here, each essay captures—from a quite distinct perspective—the joys, challenges, and impact of the Swarthmore experience. Yet across generations, geography, background, beliefs, and walks of life, these essays also speak in one voice, evidencing the consistent power of a Swarthmore education to refine intellect and wisdom, to reinforce and broaden social consciousness, and to deepen humanity. Anyone who has known Swarthmore will be moved by the profound recognition of the meaning of Swarthmore that these pages convey. And all who engage with the content of these pages will encounter a model of the means and purposes of a fine undergraduate education unmistakably validated by the qualities of persons and lives it has shaped. I invite you to live—or relive—the Swarthmore experience.

Introduction

Roger Youman '53

T*he* *Meaning* *of* *Swarthmore?* How do you define a place that has meant so many things to so many people? One way is to ask an assortment of those people to do it, in the form of brief essays. We asked, they responded enthusiastically and brilliantly, and this book is the result.

When we started this project, we knew this much: We wanted to invite 40 or 50 Swarthmore alumni to reflect on the meaning that a Swarthmore education and the Swarthmore experience have had in their lives. We wanted to hear from a broad cross-section of Swarthmoreans who have, in one way or another, made a difference in the world. We wanted the essayists to venture beyond the predictable nostalgia of a stroll up Magill Walk and down Memory Lane, and dig deeper. We asked them to reflect on Swarthmore's impact on who they are, what they have accomplished, and the way they have conducted their lives.

Since all of our writers would be products of a Swarthmore education, we had reason to feel confident that we could look forward to publishing essays that were thoughtful, lively, and provocative. Beyond that, of course, we had no way of knowing how they would answer the question posed by the book's title. Now we do know. We have a collection of 48 different—and often surprising—perspectives. In the pages that follow, they are presented chronologically (by dates of graduation).

The four dozen authors emerged from a selection process that was enormously difficult—space limitations dictated that we could accommodate no more than 50 essays, and there were too many extraordinary alumni to choose from. Hundreds of worthy candidates were considered before we ultimately settled on a group that was chosen for its balance as well as its strength—for the book itself to have meaning, it was essential to have representation from all Swarthmore generations and from a wide range of backgrounds and life experiences. The invitations went out, the replies came back, and we were gratified to receive a high percentage of acceptances. Even though we were asking accomplished people to take time out from their busy lives to write about their college—and about themselves, never easy to do—this response did not come as a surprise, because we knew how devoted to Swarthmore its alumni tend to be and how positive they feel about the role the College has played in their lives.

The lineup of essayists confirms that we achieved our goal of fielding a multifarious team of contributors. In fact, one way of viewing the book is as a demonstration of the true meaning of diversity rather than the narrow one that is used these days in simplistic political arguments. The authors came to Swarthmore from rural New Jersey and rural Bangladesh; from East Harlem and North Dakota; from Boston and Berlin; from Africa, Asia, Europe, and Latin America; and from every section of the United States. Among them are entrepreneurs, social activists, physicians, journalists, scientists, teachers, musicians, financiers, judges, a theatrical director, an Internet pundit, a U.S. senator, and a former candidate for president.

As they look back on their Swarthmore years, they summon up memories of friends, professors, College presidents, deans, coaches, classes, seminars, study groups, community work, and sports competitions that influenced their lives. And conversations—oh, those conversations! Almost every essayist makes reference to the atmosphere of talk that enveloped the campus—conversations in pairs and in groups, in dorms and dining halls, on walks and lawns, all day long and far into the night—leaving no doubt that Swarthmoreans not only thrived on the verbal give-and-take but found serious and lasting meaning in it. One essayist neatly describes the campus environment: "I was surrounded by trees and opinions."

The authors comment on the ways in which they were affected by exposure to Quaker traditions, by the small size of the student body, by the accessibility and helpfulness of the faculty and administration, by the beauty of the campus, by the sense of freedom they felt there. Underlying all of that is a theme that runs through the entire book. Although the writers find many different ways of saying it, all of them emphasize that they acquired much more than knowledge at Swarthmore, that their College experience inspired them to look beyond academics and find ways of serving not just their own interests but those of others.

The essays span nearly seven decades at the College— from the Class of '33 to the Class of '96—and touch on the most significant events and issues of those times: World War II, McCarthyism, the Cold War, the civil rights movement, the Vietnam War, scientific breakthroughs, apartheid, women's rights, capital punishment, world hunger, health care, education, journalistic ethics, even the role of diversity itself.

Swarthmore alumni have been involved in all of these developments and concerns, often in leadership positions, and the specifics in these essays provide ample evidence that they have found effective ways of serving their community and the world, and lending a hand to those who need it the most. At some stage of life after Swarthmore, the values that they had absorbed there came to the surface and led them to devote themselves to moral and social causes—justice, equality, peace, human dignity. And many of them chose unconventional and difficult ways of going about it.

A few excerpts suggest what you will find at the core of these essays:

"[Swarthmore] was a place where I got to see up close a unique face of America, full of unapologetic idealism and passion about morality, integrity, and social justice."
—*A Ghanaian member of the Class of '69 who became an international businessman*

"A cast of mind was developed that would serve one well in the years to come: not only to search for hidden truths but, having found them, to assess them in terms of their moral implications."
—*A member of the Class of '64 who became a federal judge*

"Swarthmore has never been just about ourselves. The campus culture always encouraged the use of one's education to make the world a better place."
—*A member of the Class of '66 who became an education expert*

"In some alchemical way, the calm contemplation forged iron-like commitments to seek to make the world more just."
—*A member of the Class of '74 who became a professor of law*

"The sense of responsibility for being engaged with one's own community and the wish to make it better—more just, more compassionate, more open to a wide range of people and ideas—leads me now."
—*A member of the Class of '67 who became a producer of children's television programs*

"[Swarthmore] has provided me with a model of public service that I have emulated."
—*A member of the Class of '81 who found a unique way to empower the poorest people in his native Bangladesh*

"Making a difference in the lives of one's fellow citizens is the most satisfying and the most fulfilling thing one can do during his lifetime on this planet."
—*A member of the Class of '55 who went into politics*

"To the extent that we are able to accomplish good works, the whole world is lucky that we went to Swarthmore."
—*A member of the Class of '86 who founded a boarding school for inner-city children*

That's just a taste of the rich reading experience that awaits you. So eloquently do the essays speak for themselves, nothing more needs to be said about them. The last word belongs to our authors, one of whom (Class of '78) makes an observation that speaks to—and for—all of the Swarthmoreans who so generously contributed their perceptions to the book as well as the many thousands more who will read it: "We, in all our multidimensional diversity, are the meaning of Swarthmore."

Roger Youman, former editor of TV Guide, *is a writer and editorial consultant who also teaches at the Columbia University School of Journalism. He volunteered to edit this book.*

Getting Out
the Vote

Molly Yard Garrett '33

My greatest experience at Swarthmore was organizing and leading the campaign to abolish sororities in the early 1930s. I did not know at the time that this was just the first of many political battles for me.

I got into the campaign because the sororities were unfair and discriminatory. In my class, there was a Jewish student from Chicago, Babette Schiller, who was extremely clever and talented. She wrote and produced playlets that greatly aided my sorority, Kappa Alpha Theta, in its "rushing"—persuading freshman students to join. So appealing was her work that I and several of my classmates wanted Kappa Alpha Theta to invite her to become a member. But our sorority leaders would not consider her. Was it because she was Jewish? They refused to say why.

Several other similar events occurred in the sororities. My sister Elizabeth's sorority, Chi Omega, refused to pledge her classmate Eleanor Flexner, whose father, Abraham Flexner, was an eminent fund-raiser for Johns Hopkins, and whose mother was a successful playwright. Eleanor herself became a historian who achieved stunning success as the author of *A Century of Progress*, the story of the struggle to win for women

*I did not know at the time that this was
the first of many political battles for me.*

the right to vote in the United States.

With these incidents in mind, some of us decided we should eliminate the source of such unfairness, and we organized the abolition campaign, making sure that we had representation from each sorority, as well as from women students who were left out of the system. We educated all women students on the unfairness of the sorority system and gradually got more and more of them to agree with us. The vote among women students, when it finally occurred, was overwhelmingly against women's sororities.

Several important lessons were learned from the campaign. First, we had to deal with the question of what we should have in place of the sororities, which were the lifeblood of social activities at the College. We put our heads together and decided to establish a committee of the Women's Student Government Association to plan social life for the coming year. It was a most successful decision—the WSGA did an excellent job. All students were included in the program; there was no discrimination of any kind. And we learned that we didn't need the sorority system to have a social life at college and a good time.

We also learned that the triumph that so pleased us was upsetting to some women students, who personally considered the decision a disaster. This taught us the hard lesson that one's own triumph may bring sorrow to others. So began our knowledge of the necessity of underpinning our success with compassion for the feelings of others.

One final lesson was learned from Frank Aydelotte, who was president of the College at that time. When the vote to abolish sororities was announced, many alumnae were furious. They descended on Swarthmore and demanded that the College not accept the vote. To placate them, President Aydelotte decreed that no sorority edict could take effect for a year. Now *I* was the one who was furious. We had won fair and square. Who was he to change the vote?

I rushed to the president's house, banged on the door, and demanded of him what he thought he was doing. "What's the matter, Molly?" he said. "Are you afraid to take another vote at the end of next year? Such a vote is guaranteed by my agreement with the alums." I said of course I was not afraid to take another vote. And that is what we did.

We entered into another year of hard work—educating and persuading the new students of the correctness of our position. When the vote was held, we won again, overwhelmingly.

The whole campaign was very educational for me. I devoted many years after college to social activism and political campaigns, employing many of the techniques we had learned in the campaign to abolish sororities. I worked in Philadelphia mayoral campaigns and also those for the U.S. Senate. And I was active in the presidential campaigns of Adlai Stevenson, John F. Kennedy, Hubert H. Humphrey, and George McGovern. Eventually, I ran my own campaign to become a member of the Pennsylvania legislature—unsuccessfully. I had learned in college what had to be done to get voters involved, but apparently I did not learn well enough for myself.

Molly Yard Garrett, a lifelong social and political activist, was the president of the National Organization for Women.

The Sense
of the Meeting

Sue Thomas Turner '35

My memory of Swarthmore is long. It goes back even further than 1931, when I arrived as a student. Some of my earliest memories are connected to Swarthmore. Over my father's desk hung an odd-looking object, which I learned was the lacrosse stick he used as a member of Swarthmore's 1898 lacrosse team. Down the hall hung an engraving of a benevolent-looking gentleman, Benjamin Hallowell, who was my mother's great-grandfather and also a member of the group through which Quakers from New York, Philadelphia, and Baltimore founded the College. Martha Elliot Tyson, who is considered a founder, lived nearby.

When I entered my first botany class in 1931, Dr. Palmer greeted me. "So you are Fred Thomas' daughter." My father's favorite sports area was track and field, coached by Doc Palmer.

And the memories continue all the way to the present day. It has been my good fortune to have had continuing contact with the vitality of the campus. I recall with pleasure the wonderful alumni who have served with me on alumni committees and councils, and on the Board of Managers. I have derived strength from these experiences, and I have rejoiced in the challenges. Now, limited by age, I resent the fact that I have had to miss meetings on the vibrant campus.

In 1868, when Swarthmore's first class was graduated, all members of the Board were Quakers. Nearly 100 percent of the students were from Quaker homes. In the 1930s, 25 percent were Quakers; today, fewer than that. The College was never under close control of a Quaker meeting, nor was denominational emphasis permitted. But it is clear that the Quaker search for the sense of the meeting has always been the way of conducting business, and that is what first came to mind when I thought about what I might say about the meaning of Swarthmore.

The Quakers developed a series of testimonies to support their searches for the best solution and to shore up backsliders: (1) peaceful settlement of issues—negotiation, not litigation; (2) equality of races and sexes—the Board of Managers comprised an equal number of men and women; (3) equality of educational opportunity; and (4) social concerns and service. These concerns are fully evident on all parts of the campus today, supported by Swarthmoreans from within and without.

In searching for ways to conduct affairs through the sense of the meeting, an example is reported in *Annals of Sandy Spring*, a chronicle of a Maryland Quaker community:

In 1740, one Friend said to another, "Is thee comfortable with holding slaves?" Not many days later, the slave-holding Quaker farmer said to his wife, "Sarah, I can no longer hold slaves." Forthwith, their slaves were freed (and probably given a plot of land on which a kitchen garden would provide food for a family).

This anecdote illustrates the power of seeking the right course. The Friend who asked the question placed his sense of the best way against that of the slave holder, so that more light could illuminate the situation and suggest a solution.

Over my father's desk hung the lacrosse stick he used as a member of Swarthmore's 1898 lacrosse team.

The College's 1990 *Ad Hoc Report on Governance* concluded: "We believe our Quaker tradition continues to provide a unique foundation for Swarthmore's system of governance, which seeks to find the sense of the meeting. It places responsibility on each individual to be an active participant, a conscientious listener, and have patience and sensitivity to know when to abandon a position or stand aside. We feel this process continues to result in sound positions being developed. In addition, individuals who have participated and experienced the process are better able to commit support to the position approved even if it does not reflect their own views in every aspect."

As we seek the sense of the meeting, we must recognize the danger of not taking enough time, or being controlled by agenda and by the urgency of competing viewpoints. This can slide off into a consensus that has the intent of producing a product. It usually does, but the result may be undermined by the process—or lack of process—and it may not easily bring commitment from those who are to carry it out.

The sense of the meeting solution may arrive along the way if it is the result of sharing each other's light and if the seekers are open to that light. It demands patience, and being present in the deepest sense and to the fullest extent. And it allows for healing.

Three rather explosive issues that have been part of my experience may help explain.

The first occurred in 1933, when, as a student, I was among those asked to discuss the future of women's sororities with a low-key committee of the Board. I found these infrequent meetings scary; we were dealing with an incredibly sensitive issue. As freshman adviser for the Women Students Government Association, I had observed the stress felt by those women who were not chosen for sorority membership and watched from the sidelines as a far larger group became members. The Board decided to cancel the sorority system, and we juniors became accustomed to greeting distressed alumnae on the doorstep of what had been their sorority house and was now a lodge available to the whole campus.

The next difficult issue was "open dorms." At the time, it seemed outlandish to think of men and women sharing dormitory space, but, of course, the College went ahead and created open dorms, after adjusting some facilities for privacy. I quizzed our Swarthmore-graduate granddaughter (Class of 2000). "No problem," she said. "People agree on the use of space and then live up to it."

The most explosive and dramatic issue by far was the matter of investments in South Africa. In 1986, when the members of the Board of Managers left their various committee meetings for the walk to Whittier House and the full Board meeting, we were forced to step over prone students protesting the plight of the black people of South Africa and the fact that the financial aid students were receiving was generated, in part, by South African investments. A group led by Harvard professor Christopher Edley '73 and several other Board members was determined to change the College's investment policies. (While I was collecting material for this essay and recalling these events, it was positively eerie to see Chris again—on my TV screen, where he was commenting on the Supreme Court's decision to review the admissions policies of the University of Michigan. A domestic civil rights issue this time.)

When the Board settled on divestment, one Manager resigned, and several stood aside, as the Board split over whether prudent management of entrusted funds or the issue of apartheid should take precedence. But what occurred after that is more illuminating: The Manager who resigned has never failed to support the College in every way possible and is a highly valued member of the management team. Two other Managers—one in charge of Finance and Trusts, the other of Investments—worked together to implement the decision in a way that would have minimal impact on Swarthmore's endowment. Neither had favored divestment, but they were empowered to carry it out. And it worked!

Governing the College through the sense of the meeting isn't easy, but it can work. When my husband, Bob, and I were Wednesday students at the Barnes Foundation from 1940 to 1941, Bertrand Russell was a guest lecturer. He had brought his wife and young son to the United States to escape the war in Europe, and the boy was in a Bucks County Quaker school. We often gave Lord Russell a lift to the Barnes from the Merion railroad station nearby, and, on one of these occasions, we described to him the Quaker process for seeking the sense of the meeting for decisions. After some thought, he commented, rather tartly, "I doubt if Canada and the U.S.A. would ever have reached a settlement on the future of the St. Lawrence Seaway with such a process."

When we told this story to our Quaker-nurtured children, one of them said: "But we don't know, do we? They didn't try."

I hope that present and future Swarthmoreans will carry forward the legacy of trusting the sense of the gathered participants, as they seek the solutions to whatever difficult problems they will face in the years ahead. We can be comforted by the thorough way the College has recently examined such issues as the plans for new dormitories, and we can thank our lucky stars that the current leaders of the College believe in discourse and diversity.

Sue Thomas Turner, a former member of the Board of Managers, continues to serve on Board committees.

The Meaning
Is Clear

Eugene Lang '38

Truth is stranger than fiction—so my 69-year relationship with Swarthmore affirms. Before August 1933, the name Swarthmore twice touched my awareness. First, a day in the late 1920s, when a newspaper comic strip, "Tillie the Toiler," presented a ballooned introduction of the featured working girl to an elegantly turned-out young man: "Tillie, this is Dick Van Horn of Swarthmore." I recall that, in its context, the introduction inspired the fantasy of an uppity college populated with high-society playboys. Second, some time later, when the banner headline of an article on the front page of the *Sunday Times* sports section proclaimed Swarthmore's 20-0 football victory over Army.

Neither Swarthmore reference impressed me. I had no interest in the ups and downs of a paper doll, and football was not an accredited sport on 103rd Street in East Harlem. Now, however, I wonder: Of the unending irrelevancies that stream past the senses of a young man every day, what whim of Providence preserved the two Swarthmore references in my memory bank? They did not come to mind when, by the most improbable circumstances, I met George Jackson, a sedate, unassuming gentleman who dined regularly in a small Third

> *Three years too young, and away from home for the first time, I was challenged to prove myself in a very different and formidable environment.*

Avenue restaurant where I had an after-school job as dishwasher. As it turned out, Mr. Jackson was my first exposure to a Swarthmore graduate and, auspiciously, one whose family was associated with the College back to its beginnings.

The story of that chance encounter has been told, retold, and, indeed, embellished by time. However, space allotted to this essay allows only for its conclusion. Dear Mr. Jackson, gently encouraging my interest, created a college opportunity that I considered unreal and had no intention of accepting. In January 1934, I became a 14-year-old graduate of New York's Townsend Harris High School. My credentials: advertising manager of the THH yearbook and member of its chess team. But that September, thanks to Mr. Jackson and a generous scholarship, I visited Swarthmore for the first time—as a freshman resident of Wharton's D Section. What a satisfaction it was, years later, while he was still alive, to endow the George Jackson Scholarship at Swarthmore!

A new world began to unfold. Three years too young, and away from home for the first time, I was challenged to prove myself in a very different and formidable environment. Stickball, the 79th Street library, and camaraderie in the iceman's cellar at the First Avenue corner were out, replaced by dormitory bull sessions, the "libe" (old Tarble), and "Collection" (later called "Commons") upstairs in Parrish after dinner. However, with my first 8 a.m. class in American literature with Everett Hunt, the meaning of Swarthmore began to take root. I still have my freshman-year notes that, among other pedagogical exposures, record my disputes with Emerson and Thoreau—and with Everett Hunt. Everett became a lifelong friend—I was privileged to convey my affection and respect at his 90th-birthday party in 1981 and with a eulogy at his memorial service in 1984. The Everett Hunt Room is now an important facility of the Lang Performing Arts Center.

Starting with that first 8 a.m. class, every course and seminar of my Swarthmore education opened up an opportunity to learn, to question insistently, and to challenge responses. These opportunities were immeasurably enriched by ready access to my teachers for comfort and guidance. Joining Everett Hunt in my Swarthmore pantheon are Roland Pennock, whose brilliance as a political theorist was associated with kindness and understanding that helped me cope with the profundities of his topical analyses; Brand Blanshard, whose stimulating introduction to philosophy excited active discourse of philosophic options but left my identity as a pragmatic idealist—or idealistic pragmatist—unresolved; Freddy Manning, whose eloquent expositions and special insights into American history and Constitutional issues still resonate with my perceptions of current social concerns; Mary Albertson, who made medieval history come alive and unintentionally misdirected my focus from England to the Ottoman empire; Clair Wilcox, whose social economics seminars and informal discussions, stimulated by his provocative commentaries and high-voltage student participation, were central to my major in economics; and "Uncle" George Bordelais, who generously indulged my extracurricular interest in working with the equipment in the College's engineering facilities. One of my "workings": a custom-built stepladder to facilitate postings to the baseball field's scoreboard. Over the years, this personal pantheon of faculty has become an increasingly significant and, indeed, irreplaceable, part of Swarthmore's meaning to me.

Two meaningful memories also relate to President Frank Aydelotte. First, in the second semester of my freshman year, a prominent Spanish political scientist and leader, Dr. Salvador Madariaga, was invited to give a lecture at Swarthmore. The lecture was stimulating, but there was no opportunity to ask questions. The next morning, with misgivings, I went to the President's Office and was very graciously admitted. I stated my interest in Dr. Madariaga's lecture and regretted that there had been no time for him to interact with students. With no further discussion, Dr. Aydelotte stepped out of his office for some words with his secretary. He returned and asked me, "How about tea with Dr. Madariaga at my home this afternoon at five?" I quickly agreed. He added, "If you like, you can also invite 10 other students." That blew my mind—me, a freshman, suddenly vested with such extraordinary power of patronage. Cloaking power with modesty, I invited a few of my classmates, but mostly some prominent seniors, to what became a very spirited tea. Dr. Aydelotte was that kind of president.

Four years later, on my graduation day, I was sitting on the Parrish front porch, suited up with cap and gown, waiting to assemble for the big ceremony, then held in Clothier. As I sat there, President Aydelotte came strolling by, arm in arm with the guest speaker, Professor Albert Einstein. A student, Molly Whitford, happened by with a camera and asked them to stop for a picture. They did, backing up against the side of the porch so that, coincidentally, I was framed in, to make an apparent trio. Some 30-plus years later, Molly, browsing through her files of memorabilia, found the photo, recognized me, and sent the negative. Ever since, the photo has provided a meaningful Swarthmore identity in my office, with copies on permanent display in my home and the homes of my children.

Added to this are wonderful relationships with my 1938 classmates, whose living presences and memories make them a very special and a cherished part of Swarthmore's meaning. The lengthened shadows of those classmates and, indeed, of all alumni, continue to contribute to that meaning. With them, and for seven years as chairman of the Board of Managers, I have seen the College grow in the face of wrenching challenges, ranging from curriculum, to technology, to diversity, to the Blue Route, to divestment, to football, to equal opportunity. It has been an enormous satisfaction to join with Swarthmore colleagues and participate personally, creatively, and financially in helping the College meet these challenges. We can properly take satisfaction from the widespread recognition that, in liberal arts education, Swarthmore rates at the top. However, it is significant to the meaning of Swarthmore that we remain actively aware that our college must prepare to assume new responsibilities as an academic leader in a changing world and to educate its students more effectively for socially responsible citizenship. Of colleges that have much, much is expected. The meaning of Swarthmore requires that we continue to support that expectation.

When I arrived at Swarthmore 69 years ago, I could not have imagined how meaningful the College would become in my life. I have lived to see two of my children and two of my grandchildren graduate. I dare to expect that more will have that privilege—not to mention the possibility that I may bear witness to the admission of at least two great-grandchildren. When I walk across its campus and see students immersed in themselves and each other, books under their arms, Swarthmore becomes a living spirit. Looking down Magill from the vantage of Parrish, I think of President Kennedy at the Berlin Wall, announcing, "Ich bin ein Berliner." Yes, I am a Swarthmorean—and the meaning is clear.

⚬⚬

Eugene Lang is a philanthropist, chairman emeritus of REFAC Technology and Development Corp., and a recipient of the Presidential Medal of Freedom.

Lifelong Learning

Jerome Kohlberg '46

Though my Swarthmore odyssey stretches back more than 60 years, my experiences of those times are clearly etched in my memory. I arrived at Swarthmore in July 1943, in the midst of World War II. Only six months later, I would be in a U.S. Navy officers training program on the campus. That short six-month "civilian" period colors most of my early remembrances of our College.

My first visit to the Quaker Meetinghouse on campus left an indelible impression. I recall sitting quietly for a whole half hour on its wonderful spare wooden benches, until the silence was finally interrupted by a member of the congregation reading from the funny papers while drawing pointed conclusions. The Quaker principles attracted me: Friends stood up for what they believed, didn't follow the crowd, and had a straightforward approach to others, always leaving room for understanding and forgiveness. I learned the Quaker way of mediating differences and reaching consensus. These have served me well. It also said a lot to me that Swarthmore harbored on its campus two organizations with such disparate beliefs as the Quakers and the U.S. Navy.

It was a just and human refuge in a world where the threat of military service hung over our heads.

I enjoyed the small-college sports program that offered an opportunity to participate in football, tennis, and track. There were no athletic scholarships, only eager "walk-ons," and, thanks to Coach Carl Delmuth, even a small, timorous fellow like me could make the varsity football team (third string). I roomed with Phil Evans (for whom the Evans Scholarships are named), who became my closest friend until his untimely early death. His love of music and his lust for life were infectious.

We lived in Pittinger, and I took frequent walks with Old Man Pittinger, who still stalked the campus and with whom I had many long talks. He was a wonderful source of knowledge about life and Swarthmore, and epitomized the peripheral rewards of a small college.

I struggled with physics but was enthralled by W.H. Auden, who taught English. Here we were, 10 or so freshmen, listening to one of the most distinguished poets and writers of the English-speaking world. Auden enhanced my love of literature, and, to this day, I pull books off our shelves and return to his writings and quotations. Then, as now, scholarship and teaching drove the college. The faculty, in a subtle—and sometimes not so subtle—way, taught us the rewards of serious scholarship and the pleasures to be derived from lifelong learning.

Swarthmore was an oasis of civility during this defining period of my life. It was a just and humane refuge in a world where the threat of military service hung over our heads. All these things were meaningful then; they still are today.

Rereading this, 60 years later, I am struck by the nostalgia I have for those days and reminded of how much Swarthmore has meant to me.

※

Jerome Kohlberg, a founder of Kohlberg Kravis Roberts & Co., is a partner in Kohlberg & Co., chairman of the board of the Salk Institute for Biological Studies, and chairman of the Kohlberg Foundation.

Reaching
for the Stars

Nancy Grace Roman '46

I never seriously considered any occupation other than astronomy. A piece of artwork I did when I was in third grade shows a girl gazing out the window at the night sky, next to a poem about looking at the stars. When I was 11, I organized an astronomy club among my friends. In the dark, clear skies on the edge of Reno, Nev., we met once a week during the summer to learn the constellations.

That third-grade image and poem, in a way, symbolize the meaning that Swarthmore has had for me. At a time when it was not easy for a woman to build a career as a scientist, I found in Swarthmore a place where such dreams could be translated into realities—and also a place that stimulated an interest in a variety of social problems—as well as in the humanities—that has enriched my whole life.

My choice of Swarthmore, and my years there, were influenced by the Second World War. When Pearl Harbor was attacked in 1941, I was in the first semester of my junior year in high school. In my accelerated program, I would have enough credits to graduate at the end of the junior year. Many of the girls in our small class in Baltimore (where the best public high schools were, and still are, sexually segregated) wanted to get out early to do war work or start studying for their professions. The school administration agreed—on two conditions: that all of us did it and that we would go to summer school to study a year of chemistry (in 10 weeks, with first- and second-semester chemistry taught simultaneously).

Thus, I started to choose a college earlier than I had expected and was late in applying. Because I had no brothers and had gone to a girl's high school, I wanted to go to a coeducational college. Locally, Johns Hopkins would take women only in night school, and the University of Maryland did not have a good reputation at that time. The fact that travel was difficult during wartime led me to Swarthmore because it was not too far from Baltimore, and it had a reputation for excellence and a highly regarded Astronomy Department. In contrast to the way things work today, I applied only to Swarthmore and never visited the campus or talked to an alumnus. Fortunately, I was accepted, and I have never been sorry.

The College's distribution rules required courses in the humanities and social sciences as well as math and physical science. In freshman year, I took math, astronomy, German, and history. I felt that the reason I managed to get through that year was that I did not have to spend much time studying math and astronomy. This convinced me that I was right to choose astronomy as my major, but my decision did not sit well with Dean Blanshard, who was strongly opposed to women going into science or engineering. I finally got mild encouragement in my junior year when, in lab one day, Dr. Wright said, "I usually try to discourage women from going into science, but I think maybe you'll make it."

I attended the summer session for the first semester of my sophomore year, taking first-year physics at 2 p.m. The class was composed largely of V-12 students (members of the Navy) who had been up since 5:30 a.m., when they were put

> *Near the middle of each class, he arranged*
> *some sort of noisy demonstration.*

through military drills. Predictably, the early rising, combined with the summer heat after a large lunch, had a sleep-inducing effect. Dr. Wright recognized the problem. He never said anything, but, near the middle of each class, he arranged some sort of noisy demonstration.

Although my heavy schedule of technical courses left little room for the humanities and social sciences, it was impossible not to get a liberal education at Swarthmore. The four years there left me eager for more. Since then, I have read far more broadly, and participated in groups and lectures encompassing many different interests.

I found graduate school at the University of Chicago easy compared with Swarthmore. I stayed on at the university for six years, teaching, but I recognized that, as a woman, my chances of receiving tenure were small. In 1955, I accepted a position in radio astronomy at the Naval Research Laboratory (NRL) and moved to Washington, D.C., where I have lived ever since. Radio astronomy was new in this country, although it had been developing for several years in the Netherlands, England, and Australia. I had become interested in the structure of the Milky Way and believed that radio astronomy would contribute a lot to this field—but I was too early. In those days, radio astronomers were expected to build their own state-of-the-art instruments. Although I enjoyed both the work and the group of people I was working with, I had no desire to start over as an electronic engineer.

Three years later, NASA was formed, with most of its scientists coming from NRL. I was invited to join the agency to set up a program in space astronomy. I agonized over the decision. I had enjoyed teaching and research and realized that if I took a management position, I was unlikely to get back to either. I had reluctantly left teaching; did I also want to leave research? I didn't, but the opportunity to set up a program that I believed would influence astronomy for 50 years was more than I could resist. Hence, in March 1959, I left NRL for NASA headquarters. The Hubble Space Telescope became an important part of my program.

Although I found people significantly more difficult than stars, I enjoyed the work at NASA. Nevertheless, after 21 years, I was tired of the job, and I decided to take advantage of an early-retirement opportunity. I felt too young to quit working entirely, so I found a part-time position as a consultant to a company supporting projects at NASA's Goddard Space Flight Center (GSFC) near Washington. As I wanted more work than that, I went to the Astronomical Data Center at GSFC and asked for a job, saying: "I know astronomical catalogs. If you will teach me computers, I'd like to work for you." Despite this odd approach, I got a job. I learned modern computers largely by using them and stayed there, with increasing hours, until I finally retired in 1998.

As my career shows, the greatest gift I received from Swarthmore was the ability and eagerness to learn new things. The College gave me a good background in the fundamentals of my field that permitted me to understand problems, techniques, and instruments well outside my research experience. I am the only person I know who did not have any English courses in college, but writing seminar papers was a great learning experience. I think my biggest asset in my NASA job was the ability to speak and write easily and well.

Another priceless gift from my college years was a lifelong desire to use my education in the service of others. Retirement has afforded me more time for such activities as teaching courses for high school students and science teachers, lecturing to adults on astronomy, and recording for the blind and dyslexic.

Swarthmore deserves a great deal of credit for the interesting life I have had.

❀

Nancy Grace Roman was chief of the Astronomy and Relativity programs at the National Aeronautics and Space Administration.

Two-Bluebird Nights

C. Russell de Burlo Jr. '47

June 1942 was an uncertain time for our country—and for the students entering college. We were at war with the Axis countries: Japan, Germany, and Italy.

The students of 1942 were children of the Depression, many from modest-income families like mine. No one in my immediate family had gone to college, but I was expected to go because of my strong academic record in high school and because a college degree was viewed as necessary to ensure a financially secure future.

I had two close friends—Charles Newitt '44, a sophomore at Swarthmore; and John Cookenbach '31, an alumnus—who encouraged me to go to Swarthmore for its academic program and also because they believed that I would be able to play varsity sports, which were a vital part of my life. My decision turned on the latter. This opportunity would not have been available to me at Penn, where I had been offered a full-tuition scholarship.

They were correct: I did play varsity soccer and baseball from freshman year through senior year. And what fun I had! Swarthmore's schedule for those sports was equivalent to Division I; our opponents included Penn, Princeton, Cornell,

Army, and Navy. Being part of those teams opened the door for me to become friends with teammates—and their friends, male and female—who were upperclassmen or in different majors.

When I entered Swarthmore, the College had a 12-month program: year-round classes with only two weeks off. We took five courses (with three laboratories) per semester, with classes on Saturday and labs on Thanksgiving Day. How can I best describe the intensity of that experience? Well, every night on the radio, at midnight and 1 a.m., they played a recording of Jan Pearce singing "The Bluebird of Happiness," and we had many "two-Bluebird nights." Discipline of mind, body, and planning was essential to weather every Swarthmore day.

The lessons I learned far exceeded my limited expectations. They shaped my values, my career, and my personal life. They helped me succeed in the years that followed, starting with graduate studies at Penn and at Harvard Business School. Subsequently, I was a vice president and professor at Tufts University for many years, and I served on various National Cancer Institute committees and on advisory committees of several cancer centers.

My days still are full, since two of my colleagues in the Treasurer's Office at Tufts and I started an investment-management firm with a social conscience. We are very actively involved with a number of nonprofit institutions and several Friends organizations.

For me, the most important Swarthmore lessons were fourfold. The first was the value of disciplined thought. Second, I found that hard work can be enjoyable because of the joy of learning. Those two were embedded in my values system, but the third really made a difference in my life: faculty members who were extremely generous, not only with their time but also with their willingness to take on the responsibility of helping their students develop as individuals

When I entered Swarthmore, the College had a 12-month program: year-round classes, with only two weeks off.

who would become contributing members of society. Several of these were members of the Swarthmore Monthly Meeting of Friends; one, in particular, was a great help when I was drafted into the Navy just before the end of my junior year. Samuel Carpenter wrote to me and made arrangements for me to take my junior comprehensive exams after I completed boot camp in June 1944. We continued to correspond when I was in the South Pacific, and he welcomed me back after my discharge in June 1946.

The fourth lesson was the social activism that was intrinsic to Swarthmore. The values system of the Friends was apparent, and my first introduction was the week I entered college in 1942. I attended a campus meeting in the Friends Meetinghouse, and the simplicity and quiet of the space had a lasting impact on my emotional being.

The experience with Friends that most profoundly changed my life occurred after returning for my senior year in September 1946. I started work in the College post office, where I met a co-worker, a lovely girl who, I learned during our first date, was a member of the Swarthmore Friends Meeting. She introduced me to her family and their friends. Her father, Charles Thatcher, was a Swarthmore professor and the chief financial officer of the College. Many of their friends were alumni and Friends. As I learned more about their life on campus, my direction became clear: I would become an academic and a college administrator. What a blessing it has been for me all these years!

The most significant Swarthmore blessing has been that co-worker in the College post office. Edith Thatcher '50 and

I married in the Swarthmore Meetinghouse in May 1948, and she has been my inner light ever since.

Russell de Burlo is an educator (former treasurer of and professor at Tufts University) and investment adviser (president of The de Burlo Group).

A Safe and Tolerant Environment

Lotte Lazarsfeld Bailyn '51

I arrived at Swarthmore in the fall of 1947 without ever having seen the campus. I was struck by its beauty. Coming from a midtown Manhattan apartment, I had never experienced living in an environment of woods and lawns and trees and flowers. One memory, in particular, has stayed with me. I took a music course with Professor Swan. I may have been the only student in it; I don't recall exactly. But I remember vividly that I took my final exam by myself—in the Cloisters. Could there be a lovelier setting in which to try to compose a viola suite?

The beauty of the campus was not the only early experience that has stayed with me. Having been in a coeducational high school without ever having had a date, being asked out my first weekend—and by an upperclassman at that—was a marvelous confidence booster. It was the beginning of the role that Swarthmore played in developing my self-esteem and my sense of being able to accomplish something, however small.

On the intellectual level, the independence necessitated by the honors system has paid off many times. Indeed, nothing in getting my Ph.D., or in anything I have done since, has come close to the anxiety and final sense of achievement of

Could there possibly be a more wonderful setting in which to try to compose a viola sonata?

the honors orals. I have vivid memories of a math oral where, for the first time, I found my professors, especially Professors Dresden and Brinkman, not looking at me and encouraging me on but, with heads bowed, worrying along with me. Professor Dresden was a very special person for me—so much so that when I got engaged a year later, I brought my fiancé down to meet him.

But back to those orals. In one, I felt particularly pleased that I had remembered something about the Heine-Borel theorem, only to be told afterward by Professor Dresden—in the gentlest possible way—that what I had said had been completely foolish.

Swarthmore also provided an opportunity for political engagement—nationally as well as in the affairs of the College. It helped me overcome a natural shyness and gave me experience in talking in front of groups and running meetings, and other skills I would use for the rest of my career.

All in all, it was a safe and tolerant environment in which to grow up.

One aspect of Swarthmore I began to appreciate only after I left. I never doubted the equality of men and women until I went to Harvard for my doctoral training in the Social Relations Department. There, I discovered I was not a Harvard student but a Radcliffe student and therefore not eligible for Harvard fellowships. I also discovered that there were no dorms in which I could live, that I couldn't be a resident tutor in an undergraduate house, that I couldn't enter the main college library, and that I had to enter the Harvard faculty club by the rear door. All because I was a woman.

None of this I was even aware of while at Swarthmore—perhaps naive on my part but clearly to the credit of the College. It was not until a full 20 years after my graduation, when I became the first woman faculty member at MIT's Sloan School of Management, that I began to feel as if I might approach the equality that was so easily taken for granted at Swarthmore. I must admit, though, that I still haven't reached the sense of "no problem" around this issue that I had so casually enjoyed during my College years. For this, as for so many other things, I am grateful that I decided to come to Swarthmore. It was a lucky instinct.

Finally, although I was a Jewish refugee from Austria, I had not come from a religious home. I did not get religion at Swarthmore, but I was struck by the Quaker tradition. From Collections and occasional visits to the meetinghouse I got a sense of collective integrity that impressed me. So now, as I occasionally, though not very often, think about retirement homes, it is only the Quaker ones that I would consider.

෯෯

Lotte Bailyn, an authority on conditions of the workplace, is a professor at MIT's Sloan School of Management.

The Nurturing
of a Scientist

Maxine Frank Singer '52

Nowadays, diversity in the Swarthmore student body is considered to be an essential component of a good education. And yet the Swarthmore I knew in our years was, in its own way, amazingly diverse. You wouldn't know it from looking at our yearbook photos, where all the women are wearing sweaters with pearls; and all the men, ties and jackets. In fact, the range of talents, interests, and outlooks was enormous.

Diversity is, in a very real sense, my business. I evolved from a chemist to a geneticist—of the molecular variety. The study of genetics deals with genes, chromosomes, and DNA molecules, the source of biological diversity. This science, which has advanced so dramatically in the last 50 years, can predict the color of our eyes, hair, and skin pretty well. It can tell us about our inheritance of certain diseases. However, it still can't explain why individuals in our species have such different talents and outlooks. It may well succeed in the future, but for now, the traces of cultural inheritance are more apparent than those of our biological inheritance. At Swarthmore, I inherited values and inclinations that complemented the biological inheritance and other cultural foundations that I had brought with me to the College from Brooklyn, where I went to one of those legendary, huge New York public schools that computed student averages to the fourth decimal place. Most significantly, the Swarthmore experience prepared me to join the scientific community and sustained me in that community through these long, and never easy, years.

How was it that in the 1950 Swarthmore environment, with its American middle-class roots, its deep ties to a religious tradition, and commitment to a liberal education—in the classical meaning of that term—a young person could acquire the culture of modern science? How could this civil place impart the iconoclastic skepticism, the will and skill to challenge received wisdom that are essential to the scientific enterprise? More to the point, how could this happen to a young woman at a time when the scientific community was hardly congenial to female participants?

The answers to these questions are partly general and partly specific.

For the general, two aspects of life at Swarthmore were important for the nurturing of a young scientist: freedom and optimism. For most of us, Swarthmore meant our first freedom from family, from the communities of our childhoods. It also meant the first real intellectual freedom to think on our own. And we all quickly learned that to share thoughts meant subjecting them to criticism.

Politically, Swarthmore provided an island of freedom as well, although outside the campus the ugliness of the McCarthy era was under way. Freedom of conscience, a completely new notion for me at the time, was made a reality by fellow students who, as conscientious objectors, went to jail for failure to register for the draft. Such freedoms relate only indirectly to science, but the experience of freedom is essential to the scientific venture. And for a young woman of that era, for whom traditional restrictions and expectations countered the spirit of a free mind, even the inevitably imperfect

*We talked. We fought. We borrowed sweaters
and ideas from one another.*

vision of freedom was critical.

Optimism can follow on freedom, but it also requires a level of self-confidence. It is not enough to think that "it can be done"; it is also necessary to believe that "I can do it." The path, even at Swarthmore, was not smooth. In the required freshman course in philosophy, I loved listening to Sidney Morganbesser talk—his New York accent was a piece of home—but I didn't have the vaguest idea what he was talking *about*. I had never heard the word "philosophy" until I got to Swarthmore. I was amazed that some of my classmates had not only heard of it, but could discuss philosophers and their viewpoints with apparent intelligence. It dawned on me then that to go from the "I think I can" stage to the more optimistic "I can do it" stage requires a certain level of arrogance. I began to recognize that arrogance can play a constructive role in scholarship. Competition presents related quandaries. It's only a small slide from "I can do it" to "I can do it sooner and better than anyone else." Competitiveness, like arrogance, is not always attractive, but both often motivate good science.

That's the general component of the answer to the questions I posed. What about the specific component?

In our class, the core group of serious and gifted science students was overwhelmingly made up of women—we would have said "girls." Six of us in particular were friends. We were colleagues. We were competitors. We talked. We fought. We borrowed sweaters and ideas from one another. We lived together in shifting combinations as roommates in the same dormitories. In the preceding and following classes, there were other scientifically inclined women who figured importantly in our seminars. The men in our science and math classes were themselves wonderfully talented, but there was never any reason to assume that the men were more important to the highly interactive student group, or to the professors, than were the women. And, as the four years progressed, and the classes and seminars became smaller and more advanced, the women predominated. There was not, for us, as there apparently was for so many young women of our era, any reason not to take ourselves and each other seriously. No one told us that we were unlikely. No one told us that we couldn't do what we all dreamed of doing. The invisible walls around the campus shielded us from the fact, which most people knew and we were to learn, that there was little space in the outside world for women as scientists.

It was this core of students that really educated me. Within the group, self-doubts and feelings of inadequacy might prevail, but thanks to the group, the rest of the world began to seem manageable. No doubt, we seemed odd and arrogant to some of our fellow students, which I regret, but any arrogance we displayed was not intended.

I can't say the same for professors. There was one seminar whose membership was mainly from the core. The professor seemed oblivious to the rapidly changing paradigms in biology. Alone, I, a chemistry major, would also have been oblivious, but the others taught me. Each week, the professor laid out topics and reading lists for the next meeting. Immediately after, we all met to change the agenda, make individual assignments, and help one another find the right papers. It was an extraordinarily rich seminar and for me a determinative one. Until then, traditional biology had seemed a sea of unstructured, if interesting, observations. That seminar introduced me to the possibilities of biological chemistry for helping make sense of the vast, complex, and diverse world of living things.

Was our confidence simply the construction of ambitious young women? No, not at all. The first evidence came our senior year. Sue Carver, who became a successful cardiologist, was accepted into a great medical school, even though she ruined her chances at another by telling her interviewer that his questions about her plans for marriage and family were out of order; that took guts in the spring of 1952. The other five went on to graduate school—and with National Science Foundation fellowships. That was the first year such fellowships were available. Six hundred were awarded nationwide; 32 of them went to women; five of those women were members of the Swarthmore Class of '52; a sixth, Rada Demerec, was in the Class of '51. Some of us were fortunate enough to find ourselves in graduate departments that were hospitable. Others encountered more typical troubles from their male professors. One way or another, we prevailed. We did all the things we weren't supposed to do, as well as those we were: We got degrees, we worked, we broke new ground, we published, we married, we had children. Joan Berkowitz, an inorganic chemist, built her own successful company in the field of hazardous-waste removal. Laura Maurer Roth became a professor of physics; Vivianne Thimann Nachmias, a professor of cell biology. Barbara Wolff Searle went back to mathematics and wound up working on education all over the world for the World Bank.

Swarthmore has been and remains a place where young women can get an extraordinary start in science. Swarthmore graduates, older and younger than we, have made important contributions to the modern understanding of the natural world. It is a marvelous surprise each time I encounter one of them. Astronomers like Nancy Grace Roman '46 and Sandy Moore Faber '66; biologists like Jane Kellock Setlow '40 and Carolyn Walch Slayman '58; professor of linguistics Barbara Hall Partee '61; seismologist Ines Cifuentes '75, who became my colleague in the Carnegie Institution's efforts to train elementary school teachers in Washington, D.C., to teach science effectively.

All these women have been able to contribute to the incredible scientific discoveries of the past decades. Swarthmore made it possible. And in doing that, it has played a critical role in advancing freedom and optimism for all. It is a role to celebrate!

※

Maxine Frank Singer, a microbiologist and recipient of the National Medal of Science, was president of the Carnegie Institution of Washington until her retirement in 2003.

The Real
Bottom Line

Victor Navasky '54

Murray Stedman, who taught political science my freshman year, told us that if we remembered nothing else, we should commit to memory Robert MacIver's definition of myth ("a value-impregnated belief"), contained in his textbook *The Web of Government*. I remembered something else: Murray's line about why the student-run Commons store, which dispensed hundreds of cups of coffee a day, nevertheless lost money. "Because," he said, "Swarthmore students have an anti-business bias. Put three City College business majors in charge of that store, and, in six months, they will be making money hand over fist." I told him the business about the anti-business bias was a myth, but in my case, at least, he was right. I split my honors major between political science and English literature and minored in philosophy. Economics was nowhere in sight. Business was not my business.

Forty years later, the publisher of *The Nation*, where I worked for 16 years as editor-in-chief (after a lifetime in journalism and book writing), made me an offer I should have refused and sold me the magazine for money I didn't have. For better or worse, I was now a businessman. What to do? Where to go? I remembered, from my service as alumni representative on Swarthmore's Board of Managers, that Sam Hayes III '57 was on the faculty of the Harvard Business School. He was also on the board of Tiffany & Co. Not only did he not have an anti-business bias, but he was one of the key managers of the College's investment portfolio, which that year was the No. 1 performer in the country. So I called Sam with my idea. Suppose I opened *The Nation*'s books to one of Sam's classes of brilliant M.B.A. students. Was there a way that they could turn our little company into one of those famous case studies? The problem would be simple but challenging: how to take an enterprise that has lost money for 130 years (*The Nation* went into business in 1865, the year after Swarthmore was founded) and, without changing the magazine, turn around its economics.

Gently, Sam reminded me that although he didn't see *The Nation* regularly (or irregularly either, for that matter), he suspected that his politics were not exactly *Nation* politics. But he also thought that *The Nation* might make a fascinating case study, not for the M.B.A. program but rather for a special course given for small-business owners, presidents, and CEOs who met for three weeks a year for three years. He said that although the IQ scores of M.B.A. candidates might be higher, the OPMers (Owners, Presidents, Managers) were livelier, cockier, and more experienced. I would be invited on the day *The Nation* came up for discussion. Not quite what I had in mind, but who could object to 100 free consultants?

Sam explained how the course worked, and then a diabolical smile crept over his face, and his eyes narrowed. "You know," he said, "we can do this as a case study, but whether or not we do it, you ought to consider taking this course yourself." Only good breeding, one assumes, kept him from adding, "You don't know what you're doing."

In the end, Sam agreed to make *The Nation* a case study, and I agreed to enroll in the OPM course, where the palpable

> *Only good breeding, one assumes, kept him from*
> *adding, "You don't know what you're doing."*

sense of intellectual self-discovery that reverberated among my classmates was reminiscent of nothing so much as a Swarthmore seminar. Although I had many spirited debates with my classmates about unions, the free market, and supply-side economics—for most of them, the bottom line was still the bottom line—in the process I learned all of the practical things that Clair Wilcox never taught us in Economics 101. But I was reminded, in case I had ever forgotten, that at the Swarthmore I remembered, doubts about bottom-line thinking were often illuminated by the inner light emanating from the student sitting in the next carrel, the year was divided into seasons rather than quarters, and whether the gingko trees were still standing meant more to me than whether the yen was falling.

Maybe another way to say it is that there is the bottom line, and there is the party line. But at Swarthmore, there were no lines, unless one counts the Media-Wawa local line. Instead, Swarthmore did its best to imbue us with a critical spirit that questioned all lines, as it encouraged us to seek the good, the true, and the beautiful; to speak truth to power; to put human values above financial ones.

There are no neat morals here, but I guess it's fair to say that business values and political values both seem to be trumped by Swarthmore values.

Victor Navasky is owner, publisher, and editorial director of The Nation; *author of books and articles; and professor of journalism at Columbia University.*

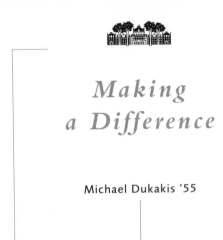

Making
a Difference

Michael Dukakis '55

I was certainly interested in politics and public affairs when I arrived at Swarthmore in the fall of 1951, but I don't think I had ever seriously considered running for public office. Swarthmore and Sen. Joseph McCarthy of Wisconsin did that for me.

Swarthmore and Joe McCarthy? That's not a pair we often associate with each other. In fact, Swarthmore was such a hotbed of anti-McCarthy sentiment during the 1950s that a ticket agent at the suburban train station in downtown Philadelphia used to refer regularly to Media as "the stop after Moscow." But those were the days when McCarthy was running around the country accusing countless Americans of being "pinkos," "crypto-Communists," or, at the very least, "Communist dupes." And I, a young kid from Boston who had been out of New England only once, found myself in a community of scholars, students, and activists that took McCarthy on and, with the help of a lot of other people, beat him.

That wasn't the only thing that was happening in and around the Swarthmore campus in 1951. The barber shops in the borough of Swarthmore wouldn't cut the hair of a hand-

I found myself in a community of scholars, students, and activists that took McCarthy on and, with the help of a lot of other people, beat him.

ful of black students who began attending the College in the late 1940s and early 1950s. Long before the civil rights revolution, Swarthmore students decided to boycott the barber shops. I became the campus barber and learned an important lesson: One could combine a commitment to social justice with economic opportunity and win on both counts.

Moreover, Swarthmore opened up opportunities for people like Carl Levin and me not only to attempt to provide leadership in such political organizations and causes as the Students for Democratic Action and the American Civil Liberties Union, but also to get actively involved in local campaigns. I was working in the river wards of Philadelphia for Joe Clark and Richardson Dilworth in the fall of 1951, as they sought successfully to oust a Republican city machine that had controlled Philadelphia for decades. We got actively involved in county campaigns as well; although Democrats weren't going anywhere in Delaware County in those days— in fact, another Republican machine controlled the county— it was great experience and whetted our appetite for more.

Throw in a summer in Peru, courtesy of the Peaslee Fellowships that were endowed by a Swarthmore alumnus, and a fall semester during my senior year at American University in Washington, and the somewhat naive lad from Boston was, by the time he graduated in June of 1955, a very different person from the one who had arrived on campus four years earlier.

Of course, campus life itself, both inside and outside the classroom, had a huge impact on me. I had only a vague idea of what a Quaker was when I first arrived, and I knew virtually nothing about the kind of work for peace in which Quakers and the colleges they had founded were so deeply engaged.

I started out as a tentative premed; got what can only be described as a charitable D in physics; and decided that political science, history, and economics were the things I really wanted to study. And I had the good fortune to do honors and to stretch my brain and think about the great issues of the day with teachers who loved to teach and knew their students well.

I've been involved in public life one way or another ever since, and I haven't regretted a day of it—except, perhaps, for Election Day in 1988. These days, I do a lot of teaching, seeking to inspire young people to become deeply and actively involved in the politics and public life of their communities, states, and country.

In a sense, I guess, I am trying to do for them what Swarthmore did for me—help them to understand that making a difference in the lives of one's fellow citizens is the most satisfying and the most fulfilling thing one can do during his life on this planet.

ॐ

Michael Dukakis, the former governor of Massachusetts and Democratic candidate for the presidency in 1988, now teaches at Northeastern University and UCLA's School of Public Policy.

Speaking Truth
to Power

Carl Levin '56

Because my four years at Swarthmore were so wonderful and my career has been so richly rewarding, looking back for experiences at Swarthmore that influenced my career is a pleasantly nostalgic experience. Of course, such a journey reinforces my awareness of the most important impact Swarthmore had on me, which, although not directly influencing my career, perhaps affected my very being: the personal relationships with classmates and professors that broadened my horizons, deepened my understanding, and enhanced my self-esteem. But, having traveled a political road, I have chosen to describe some experiences that are more political than personal. Because of my strong love for Swarthmore, an element of subjectivity no doubt suffuses my recollection of these events.

In 1954, Sen. Joseph McCarthy was riding high, intimidating our nation with his scare tactics and his attacks on our political freedoms. His excesses included both abusing the unique subpoena power he had as chairman of the Senate Permanent Subcommittee on Investigations and pillorying people who exercised their Fifth Amendment privilege before his subcommittee.

A resolution censuring Sen. McCarthy was introduced in the Senate, and the country became embroiled in the debate preceding the vote. McCarthy's supporters around the country launched a petition drive opposing the censure and planned on delivering a million signatures to our nation's capital. Some of my classmates and I decided to solicit signatures supporting the censure of Sen. McCarthy. We collected about a thousand signatures in the Swarthmore dining room in just a few days. We then drove down to Washington in our old jalopy, to deliver our petitions to Sen. James Duff of Pennsylvania.

By chance, we arrived on the same day the million pro-McCarthy signatures were delivered in an armored truck. Newspapers across the country carried two pictures side by side. One picture showed armed guards, guns drawn, delivering the pro-McCarthy petitions. Next to it was the photo of six cherubic-looking Swarthmore students exercising their right to petition their senator. David wounded Goliath in a media battle that was unplanned and lucky.

We learned an important lesson about how massive resources in politics can sometimes be countered by a relatively small-scale effort. It also taught us about the role of dumb luck in politics (one I've seen repeated time and time again!).

The censure petition was adopted by the Senate, in part because of the courage of some senators in McCarthy's own party. That vote illustrated how important it can be at times to differ with the majority of one's own party, if the merits dictate, and in doing so, how the direction of a nation can be affected.

Ironically, history placed me, for the second half of 2001 and all of 2002, in the same position Sen. McCarthy held when we delivered those petitions—at the helm of the Senate Permanent Subcommittee on Investigations. When investigating the activities of Enron, Chase, Citibank, and Merrill Lynch

> *We learned an important lesson about how massive resources in politics can sometimes be countered by a relatively small-scale effort.*

(issuing subpoenas, watching the witnesses before me "take the Fifth"), I often thought of how Sen. McCarthy abused the powers now at my disposal, and it sensitized me to the potential for abusing power, as well as using it for the public good.

A second political event that occurred in 1954 was the fall of North Vietnam to the Communists, who had defeated the French. Most of the University of Hanoi, faculty and students alike, picked up and fled south to Saigon in the hope of maintaining their academic freedom. (The Vietnam War, in which the United States would became deeply involved, was not yet on the horizon.) Several classmates and I, with students from a few nearby colleges, decided to hold a book drive to help stock a library that had to be built from scratch in Saigon. We collected thousands of books and raised the funds to ship them to Vietnam. That Swarthmore experience reinforced a belief I had long held that Americans are willing to help those in need around the world. American ideals and idealism are powerful tools for good, under the right leadership, and are readily available to be called on for great causes, such as addressing hunger or the AIDS epidemic.

A third experience involved Collection. Several classmates and I objected on principle to being required to attend that long-standing weekly event with, as it appeared to some, its quasi-religious origin and nature. Of course, many of the programs at Collection were interesting, and we wished to attend those on a voluntary basis. There apparently had not been a protest like ours before (for good reason, perhaps, given the innocuous nature of Collection most of the time). The dean came up with what he believed was a shrewd and appropriate verdict: It would be "all or none." In other words, if we wanted to skip the programs we objected to or found uninteresting, we would have to pay the price of not being able to attend the programs we wanted to attend. We readily chose the "none" option.

We had spoken truth (at least in our eyes) to power (in everybody's eyes) and "won." I believe that attendance at Collection was made optional at some point thereafter.

I have often thought of that incident and how Swarthmore reacted with such reasonableness to our proclamation of principle. But more to the point of this remembrance, I believe I have been more willing to "take on" the powerful because of the lessons learned at Swarthmore about effecting change by not being afraid to challenge the status quo.

On the one hand, these events sprang from youthful exuberance and the idealism that young people have, believing that they can change the world for the better. On the other hand, I have realized over time that these events really did influence my career, demonstrating as they did that individuals can advance causes and that the effort to do so has meaning. My years at Swarthmore shaped my life in immeasurable ways, just as it has affected the lives of almost everybody who was lucky enough to have been exposed to Swarthmore's love of learning, its respect for differences, and the obligation to all life on our fragile planet that it seeks to instill.

Carl Levin is a U.S. senator from Michigan and the ranking Democrat on the Senate Armed Services Committee.

A Minor Major

Peter Schickele '57

Now, your old Quakers were not known for their interest in music, and the legacy of that attitude was still evident when I arrived at Swarthmore in 1952. The Music Department consisted of Alfred Swan, who also taught at Haverford, and I was the only music major. For some reason, music composition was the only applied art course offered in those days, and I took Dr. Swan's composition "course" (there were so few students in the class that it was more like a seminar) every semester I was at Swarthmore, which gave me that much more time to write.

But though music making at the College was amateur, it was intense: I sang in the chorus, played bassoon in the orchestra, helped organize a chamber music concert in Bond almost every Sunday afternoon; and when I wrote a violin concerto for my fellow student Carl Berger, I didn't have to worry about keeping the solo part easy; like many doctors-to-be, Carl was a serious musician. I wrote (and—this is important—*heard*) four orchestral pieces and dozens of chamber works while I was there (not to mention the score for the 1957 *Hamburg Show*). The College even came up (by dipping into some lecture fund, as I recall) with some money to help get

My research into the life and music of P.D.Q. Bach would not have had the truly flabbergasting cultural depth it evinces, had it not been for the broad general education I received on the banks of the Crum.

the orchestral parts for the violin concerto copied.

The point of these anecdotes is that even though Swarthmore's curriculum was hardly set up with music in mind, so many music lovers existed among the faculty and students that there was always something going on, and, perhaps most important, the College had the flexibility to make sure that what should happen happened, even if it wasn't in the catalog. Also, it seems obvious that my research into the life and music of the putative composer P.D.Q. Bach would not have had the truly flabbergasting cultural depth it evinces, had it not been for the broad general education I received on the banks of the Crum.

Sometime during my junior year, a well-known composer agreed to look at several of my compositions; his advice was to transfer, immediately, to a school that took music seriously. I didn't take his advice, and it's true that when I graduated, it was extremely important for me to go to a real conservatory. But it's also true that, as a student at Juilliard, I was glad I'd been to Swarthmore.

Peter Schickele, composer, musician, and author, is best known for his satiric performances of the works of P.D.Q. Bach.

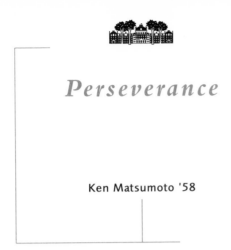

Perseverance

Ken Matsumoto '58

Never give up. Never, never, never!" This has been my motto ever since my college days. I learned this lesson of perseverance at Swarthmore through my struggle with the almost insurmountable volume of assigned reading and papers I had to contend with. Since I could not read English fast enough, I could barely complete assignments for the classes, but I continued to work hard enough to graduate. In fact, I stayed up so late, "hitting the books," that I became notorious for cooking spaghetti at 2 a.m. in the dormitory hall, where a hot plate was available.

Coming from Japan, I had expected to encounter cultural differences, but when I became a part of the College community, I was grateful for the tolerant attitude and patience of my fellow students. And I was impressed by the diversity of their views and their willingness to express them freely at any time and in any place—classrooms, dining hall, dormitory, anywhere. As I listened to them, I found myself becoming more open-minded and accepting of other people's opinions and positions. And now, later in life, I cannot imagine that I would have developed my deep appreciation of the values of people of different cultural, ethnic, and national backgrounds

There were always people who kept encouraging me to keep going and not give up.

without the experiences I had at Swarthmore.

I came to know many students who were really gifted. Because I felt almost overwhelmed by their potential, the career I envisaged for myself was not as a scholar or a researcher but rather as a coordinator of such talented people. And that is the way it has worked out. At the Fair Trade Center, a research NGO (nongovernmental organization associated with the World Trade Organization), I am responsible for the coordination of programs that bring together people of different nationalities—law professors, international bureaucrats, and specialists in the fields of international trade and economic law—and facilitate communication among them.

At Swarthmore, I acquired analytical abilities and research skills and learned how to deal with new situations. Spending four years in such an intellectual atmosphere prepared me to view things more critically and from a broader perspective. More important, I received encouragement and developed the confidence to face challenging new tasks. In my years at the College, I became more tenacious. And what I learned about the processes of learning itself has served me throughout my lifetime.

I must admit, however, that it was not until some 20 years after my graduation that I really began to appreciate the value of my Swarthmore experiences. That's when the Fair Trade Center was established. At this research institution, we analyze legal issues of trade and work to promote trade liberalization under the aegis of the GATT Treaty and the World Trade Organization. Although I had little knowledge of the field previously, I found that I could handle the new tasks better than I had expected. I came to the realization that Swarthmore had provided me with the ability to cope with this unfamiliar and demanding new situation—not through any specific courses, but through its academic demands, and the dynamic and flexible spirit of its community.

A few years ago, with the cooperation of several college professors and interested businessmen, I organized a small study group to address the problems of liberal arts education in Tokyo. Even though the task is formidable, I want to make an effort to share with Japanese colleagues the benefits that I received at Swarthmore. The situation of Japanese undergraduate education is critical, and I hope we can make a modest contribution.

For me, the unique aspects of Swarthmore are its combination of liberal intellectuality, concerns about all kinds of people, and the pursuit of justice in the Quaker tradition. There were times when I spent an hour in the silence of the Quaker meeting on campus on Sundays. I was impressed with the Quakers' pacifist beliefs and actions, including declaring themselves conscientious objectors during the period of conscription for military service. I was left with a deep respect for Quakerism. Many years later, in 1979, when I decided to be baptized, I know I was influenced by my exposure to the Quakers and their tradition. I have been active in my church, which has a Presbyterian tradition, and perhaps I have been instrumental in a modest way in advancing the religious beliefs of others.

There were many occasions during my four years at Swarthmore when I felt truly desperate. I thought I would never be able to keep up with the classes and seminars. But there were always people like the late Professor Paul Beik of the History Department who kept encouraging me to keep going and not give up. As my course adviser throughout the four years, he helped and supported me in so many ways. Without his caring and his invaluable advice, I would not have made it. There were several other members of the faculty, as well as my roommates in Wharton Hall and other fellow students, who supported me in immeasurable ways. And outside the campus, there were American families who treated me as part of their family. I owe so much to those people. What they taught me has helped me to become a helpful person to others.

For 10 years, at the request of the College's Admissions Office, I have been interviewing Japanese applicants. This task has prompted me to read College publications carefully, as well as relevant books about liberal arts education. I feel so strongly about the superiority of a Swarthmore education, in comparison with what is available elsewhere in the United States, I try to persuade the best students to choose Swarthmore, even though other institutions may offer larger scholarships or more familiar names. I am pleased that the students who have chosen Swarthmore, even though they had other options, have invariably been happy with their decision.

I was moved by the inaugural address of President Alfred H. Bloom in 1992, in which he emphasized the importance of ethical concerns in intellectual life. I have received invaluable encouragement from him and from faculty members and students whenever I return to the College campus. They make me feel that I am truly a member of the campus community. All of us alumni should feel—and can feel—that we continue to be a part of this exceptional community throughout our lives.

I now serve on the board of trustees of the Grew Foundation, which grants scholarships to Japanese high school graduates. They usually go to colleges in the United States, and I am deeply grateful that Swarthmore has, so far, accepted six Grew Scholars. One of those fortunate young people was me.

As a result, Swarthmore has been, along with my religious beliefs, the most vital factor in my life.

⚬⚬

Ken Matsumoto, who lives in Tokyo, is an adviser and trustee of the Fair Trade Center, which he directed for 10 years.

The View
from West of
the Rockies

Mary Murphy Schroeder '62

For me—and I suspect for the entire generation of middle–20th-century Swarthmore students who went into law, public policy, and public service—the College was J. Roland Pennock. No one taught constitutional law as well as Roland; no one taught students as well as he did. A man of gigantic intellectual reach himself, he understood the capacities—and the limitations—of his students.

It was because of Roland that I was able to attend a law school of the first rank. In need of hefty financial aid—and lacking the stellar academic record to obtain it easily—I set my eye on a scholarship from the University of Chicago that was specifically earmarked for a Swarthmore student. Roland watched with what I hoped was silent approval as I encouraged all of those with better records than mine to go to other law schools. He then chaired the committee that awarded me the scholarship. It was a win–win situation for just about everyone. Years later, the parent of one of the students whose legal career was influenced by my maneuverings introduced me at a Rotary Club function. He proudly called me "the person who caused my son to go to the University of Michigan Law School."

It is because of professors like Roland Pennock that Swarthmore is justifiably proud of its tradition of teaching. I am certain that there have been many professors who, like Roland, are not just teachers but career mentors. He must have followed the careers of nearly all of his students, for I recall that years after my graduation, when I was working at a law firm in Phoenix, Roland called me out of the blue. He told me that he was attending the meeting of a learned society in Phoenix and invited me to come and have lunch so that he could introduce me to his colleagues. I was floored.

Roland Pennock was the first great mentor in my life. The second was John Frank, the legendary Phoenix lawyer who, among other things, represented Ernesto Miranda in *Miranda v. Arizona*. By this time, I have myself mentored a generation of law clerks who now occupy significant positions ranging from copyright counsel for Major League Baseball to governor of Arizona. They are all, indirectly, protégés of Roland Pennock.

For many of us, Swarthmore was rough going for a few years. The salvation, though, for the uprooted midwestern freshman at Swarthmore, was the friendships. Some that we thought would last for life turned out not to, but others—especially those forged in common intellectual or professional interests—are still important.

Overall, the daily presence of members of the opposite sex in our classes, on our walks, at meals, in the library, and, yes, in our dorm rooms was exhilarating. In the era when the great Ivy League universities were for men and the "Seven Sisters" were for women, Swarthmore's co-education was the reason many of us chose it in the first place. I am convinced that it is the reason many of us succeeded in a world where men and women work together. If there is one aspect of my Swarthmore experience that I did not fully appreciate at the time but have come to value now, it was living in a world where one was judged on one's own merits, without regard to

I know that I am not alone in believing that Swarthmore helped me achieve more than I ever thought possible.

gender. I was to learn all too abruptly, entering law school as one of only five women in a class of 160, that the rest of the world fell far short of that Swarthmore ideal. It was my Swarthmore experience that inspired my later successful efforts as a lawyer to write and pass the first Arizona statute barring sex discrimination in employment, yet we still have a long way to go. Now, as chief judge of the nation's largest federal circuit, I am one of only a handful of women who sit on the governing body of the federal courts, the Judicial Conference of the United States.

Then, there was the music. Always an enthusiastic, if untutored, participant in choral music, I had a tryout with Peter Gram Swing. A marvelously dedicated musician and—this being Swarthmore—a gifted teacher, he knew after approximately 90 seconds that I was unable to repeat a sequence of more than two notes. Nevertheless, he let me into the big chorus, where I spent a wonderful two years perched precariously on the next-to-last riser of the overly large second-soprano section. The musical highlight of my life was singing on the stage of Philadelphia's Academy of Music with the Philadelphia Orchestra as a member of the combined Swarthmore, Bryn Mawr, and Haverford choruses, conducted by Eugene Ormandy. The most memorable introduction I ever heard was given at the dress rehearsal by the associate conductor, William Smith: "Mr. Ormandy is the greatest conductor in the world when he is in trouble, and, this afternoon, you are going to see him at his very best."

No institution is perfect, and Swarthmore is no exception. There is a certain parochialism inherent in being a small, coeducational college 11 miles from Philadelphia. For those of us who made our careers and raised our families west of the Rockies, Swarthmore has kept its distance. Many of us would love to be asked to come back and speak to the students and young alumni about what we learned from our Swarthmore experiences. That is the major reason I felt honored to be asked to contribute to this book. It is my hope that it will reflect the dazzling diversity of interests and achievements realized by Swarthmore alumni in many places and fields.

I know that I am not alone in believing that Swarthmore helped me achieve more than I ever thought possible when I was at the College. When I am asked why, my response goes like this: "At Swarthmore, I felt I had to run to keep up with everyone there. After I left Swarthmore, I kept the same pace and discovered I was running faster than just about everybody else." I am grateful.

Mary Murphy Schroeder, Chief Judge of the 9th U.S. Circuit Court of Appeals, has served on that court since 1979.

Teachers

Bennett Lorber '64

I am a teacher. I didn't set out to be one, but of all my professional activities in academic medicine—including caring for patients, performing research investigations, and writing scholarly papers—it is teaching that has brought me the greatest stimulation, satisfaction, pleasure, and pure joy. My path to teaching began at Swarthmore, but it wasn't my idea.

During my junior year, I took Invertebrate Zoology with Professor Norman Meinkoth. He was organized, erudite, meticulous, and clear. He could lecture while simultaneously drawing complex illustrations on the board with amazing speed. He often had a little grin, and a twinkle in his eye, which made me think he knew some special secret the rest of us could never share. He was completely without pretense and had a good sense of humor; both of these qualities are reflected in the unconventional last word of the title he picked for his book: *The Audubon Society Field Guide to North American Seashore Creatures*. Like most of my Swarthmore teachers, he assigned readings for his classes as though his was the only class we were taking. His expectations were high, and we admired him so much that we strove to meet them.

One of the course requirements was that each student had to give a formal presentation to the class, and one morning, with a lot of anxiety, I gave mine. Later that day, as I was crossing the campus, I heard my name called. I turned to find Professor Meinkoth walking toward me. He approached, put his hand on my shoulder, and said: "I know you're planning to go to medical school, but I hope that, whatever you do in medicine, you will make time for teaching. You have a gift for it." I muttered an embarrassed thank you, and we parted. Twelve years later, after medical school, residency, fellowship in infectious diseases, and two years as a medical school faculty member, I received an award for teaching. About a month later, I got a postcard on which was written: "I remember telling you in Invertebrates you should be a teacher. Congratulations! Norm."

I had several great teachers at Swarthmore, and their lessons have been invaluable. From them, I learned how to ask a question and to question authority. I learned how to present and respect a good argument. I learned to speak up when confronted by injustice and unfairness. I learned the excitement that can come from learning and the educational value of a good story. And I learned the importance of a kind word passed from teacher to student.

When I think back on the best educational experiences in Swarthmore classrooms, the subjects are inseparable from the teachers: Aesthetics with Beardsley, American Literature with Hoffman, English Literature with Hynes, Invertebrate Zoology with Meinkoth, Greek Literature in Translation with North, Neurophysiology with Rawson, Design in Drawing and Painting with Rhys, Medieval Art with Williams.

My Swarthmore professors have been the models I've drawn on to develop my own pedagogic methods and style. To this day, they provide inspiration and guidance. On occasion, when called upon to give a lecture that I've given many times, I think about making it easy on myself and giving the

> *I learned the importance of a kind word*
> *passed from teacher to student.*

same talk I gave last time. But then I remind myself that Meinkoth never took shortcuts or the expedient path, and I work to make the talk new and fresh.

Fifteen years after my graduation, I attended a dinner at the College in honor of Norman Meinkoth, who had spent his entire professional life at Swarthmore and served on the faculty for 31 years. The room was filled with well-wishers, almost all of them former students. Several had achieved great distinction in the world of biology. All had been pushed, nurtured, and encouraged by Norm. After dinner, former students representing the span of his career offered wonderful reminiscences. At the end of the evening, Norm was told he could have the last word and was asked if there was anything he'd like to say. He replied: "Just this. When I was finishing my graduate-school work, my adviser called me to his office and said: 'Norm, you're a bright boy, but you're no genius. If you're smart, you'll get a job at a good college and stick with it.' Well, I did it, and I'm glad." So am I.

※

Bennett Lorber, an authority on anaerobic infections and food-borne diseases, is chief of the Section of Infectious Diseases at Temple University School of Medicine and Hospital.

The Ghost Lives

Jed Rakoff '64

The 1960 edition of the Wentworth and Flexner *Dictionary of American Slang* defined "bull session" as "[a]n informal and often lengthy conversation, frequently idle or boastful, on a variety of topical or personal subjects, especially among a group of male students." (By 1986, in keeping with grade inflation and political correctness, the definition had improved to "[a] discussion, especially one among good companions passing time idly but investigating important topics.") Although Swarthmore in the early 1960s was filled with political activity—the historical significance of which becomes more evident with each reunion—what I most remember, not in specifics but in importance, were the nightly bull sessions, beginning no earlier than 11 p.m. (when the possibility of completing the next day's reading assignments had faded beyond hope) and ending no earlier than 2 a.m. (when the need for sustenance from the all-night diner on Baltimore Pike overrode the Search for Truth).

The Search for Truth is, of course, the purpose of bull sessions, as any college student with intellectual pretensions would be happy to tell you. As captured by that great midcentury philosopher and mathematician Tom Lehrer, they consist of:

> *Hearts full of youth,*
> *Hearts full of truth,*
> *Six parts gin and one part vermouth.*

But at Swarthmore, we could not escape that other dreaded dimension: values, especially social values. It was not enough to arrive at truth alone, for truth without values was valueless. With hindsight, what passed for truth now seems like self-delusion, and what passed for values now seems like self-importance, yet a cast of mind was developed that would serve one well in the years to come: not only to search for hidden truths but, having found them, to assess them in terms of their moral implications.

And so I became a federal judge and find that, every once in a while, I am called upon to make use of that Swarthmore training.

For example: No legal system easily accepts the proposition that its truth-finding processes are deficient. Determining the facts after-the-fact may be no easy task, but the meting out of justice so depends on it that lawyers, judges, and people generally have an almost compulsive need to believe that the truth-determining rules and procedures developed over centuries by the Anglo-American system of justice really do work. Even so great a judge as Learned Hand, sitting in the court in which I now sit, thought that, if anything, our legal system overly protected the criminal defendant: "Our procedure has always been haunted by the ghost of the innocent man convicted. It is an unreal dream." (*United States v. Garsson,* 291 F. 646, 649 [S.D.N.Y. 1923]).

Yet the ghost lives, for in the last 10 years, DNA testing has proven conclusively that scores of criminal defendants found guilty beyond a reasonable doubt were, in fact,

> *We could not escape that other dreaded dimension: values, especially social values. It was not enough to arrive at truth alone, for truth without values was valueless.*

innocent. Considering the implications of this unwanted truth for the death penalty, I came to the conclusion that, by forever depriving a convicted person of the possibility of someday proving his innocence, the death penalty denies due process and hence is unconstitutional. In so holding, I had no illusions but that, in the short run, this unpalatable conclusion, though legally correct, would nonetheless be overridden on appeal—and it was. But for me to have decided otherwise would have been either to deny the truth or to place no value on it. Consistent with my Swarthmore education, I had no choice.

๛

Jed Rakoff has been a U.S. District Judge for the Southern District of New York since 1996.

Friendly
Persuasion

Josef Joffe '65

How did this 18-year-old from Cold War Berlin get to Swarthmore? *Cherchez la femme.* The *femme* in this case was Janice, a sophisticated 17-year-old exchange student from Grand Rapids, Mich. "Sophisticated" in those days meant black turtle necks, tweed skirts, and Benson & Hedges cigarettes (the real kind, from Britain). She wrote poetry and played Joan Baez songs on the guitar; in the Midwest of the early 1960s, then still firmly lodged in the '50s, she was the epitome of hip. And she had applied to Swarthmore. "Swarthmore? Never heard of it." She brought me a pack of articles, all of which said pretty much the same things: supercharged academics, bad football, grungy clothes, and left-wing politics.

The kid from Wall Town applied, along with Janice. Of course, she did not get in (her fate was Oberlin), but he did—with an SAT score of 1,240, to boot. The number of applicants from Germany must have been a bit on the low side. So, in the fall of 1962, he was heading for that mythical point "11 miles southwest of Philadelphia," two suitcases and one portable Olivetti (the mechanical precursor of the laptop) in hand. It was the best decision he ever made.

Why? The 1960s surely were the heyday of liberal arts education in America. Though it was left-wing politics outside the Swarthmore classroom, it was the most rigorous kind of education inside. We had middle-of-the-road professors (complete with pipes and patches) who kept us intellectually honest; "commitment," "feeling," or "authenticity" did not pass as a substitute for a stringent argument. They let us take over Chester's city hall for now long-forgotten causes, but jail was no excuse for an unfinished seminar paper. "Say you want a revolution?" as the Beatles would later sing. First, you had to show up for that grueling five-hour seminar on Modern Political Theory, where Marx and Lenin were subjected to "bourgeois" rules of evidence, such as factuality and consistency.

Somehow, those all-nighters that studded a 60-hour study week also left time for writing for *The Phoenix*, organizing folk festivals and student conferences, acting in the Hamburg Show, pressuring the administration into relaxing "visiting hours," and contributing to worthy social causes off-campus. (Sex was strictly verboten.) The purpose of this romantic tale is not to sentimentalize the days when "giants walked the earth" but to stress a larger point that transcends generational bragging. At its best (and Swarthmore was the best), liberal arts education in America was a wondrous experience that built not only the mind, but also soul and character. Even with political activism on the rise, "relevance" was a term rarely applied to "education," and courses with "interdisciplinary" in front and "studies" in the tail were not yet in vogue. At any rate, Swarthmore beat attending Berlin or Munich U., vast urban universities replete with anonymity, anomie, and aimlessness.

To elucidate the general point, here are three examples.

1. Putting Descartes Before the Course

My first encounter with philosophy occurred in the

For this escapee from Cold War Berlin, Swarthmore was a wondrous bildungsroman that recorded the growth of mind, soul, and character.

introductory course given by Richard Brandt. The paper topic was "Compare Descartes and Leibniz on the Mind-Body Problem." Deferentially, I sidled up to the professor with a request for secondary sources. "What for?" "Well, before I write this paper, I need to know what the greats before me had to say." "No, you don't. You are just as good as they are. Stick to the originals, and forget the exegesis."

"You are just as good as they are...." What does an 18-year-old know from the mind-body problem? Not enough. Or just enough for a C-, as the grade would later indicate. But had the good professor, author of a standard work on ethics, steered him wrong? Not really. Because knowledge is a discovery every generation must make on its own; it is an adventure that cannot be experienced secondhand. Education is not regurgitation (as, *au fond*, in France), nor footnote flaunting (as in Germany). It is "hands on," intellectually speaking, or, more precisely, "brains on." Your *own* hands and brains.

Only your own brains? This tale offers yet another moral. When I asked what I had done wrong to deserve a C-, Brandt replied laconically: "Nothing. The others were just better." The "others" are another great secret of a Swarthmore education. As they say, and rightly so: "Fifty percent of a good education is the other students." These other "turkeys" ("Swatties," as they are called today) are the lead runners in the long-distance race that is a liberal arts education. They set the pace and the example, making the laggards wheeze, pant, and sweat until the last shall be the first (or, at least, reach the middle of the pack). Such races are not run in the anonymous mass universities of Europe, let alone in such abodes of virtual education as the University of Phoenix. In other words, a slice of my tuition rightfully should have gone to my fellow students.

2. The Seminar Syndrome

One year later, despite his so-so performance in philosophy, this student was allowed to join the Honors Program. "Classic Honors," as configured then, was ungraded and lectureless. It consisted of two afternoon-filling seminars plus one paper per week—until that Judgment Day two years later when outside examiners took the intellectual measure of Swarthmore's would-be laureates.

Two long years and one 8-to-10-page paper per week. One day, this philosophy acolyte showed up in his Aesthetics seminar (run by the legendary Monroe Beardsley, he of the "intentional fallacy") without his paper in hand. The applause for this act of insouciance was a bit weak because his essay was to be the core of the seminar—for each participant to read and scrutinize. But the only object of scrutiny was this squirming reprobate. Nobody carped or complained. His fellow students just looked disappointed. It was as if a soldier had shown up in the trench without his rifle—virtually a form of intellectual treason.

Needless to say, this happened only once in my Swarthmore career. On that afternoon, I understood that education is not an academic variant of consumerism, let alone a lifestyle choice for that hiatus between childhood and adulthood known as "I don't know what I'm gonna do." On that day, the full meaning of the ancient university *communitas*, the community of teachers and learners, was quietly driven home. Such a pedagogical wake-up call is rare in America's huge state universities and even more so in their European counterparts, where a "seminar" can easily run to 50 or 60 students. Whence it follows that a Swarthmore education is a sheer privilege, and not the kind of parking lot between high school and unemployment that so many European mass universities have become. Shall we do away with this grueling privilege in the name of equality? A look at the Sorbonne or at the Universities of Hamburg and Rome, where admission is open and tuition nil, unequivocally says "No!"

3. Quakers and Citizens

Like many American colleges, Swarthmore's roots are denominational. Though the College is now thoroughly secular, the Quaker spirit was still very much present in the 1960s. One practical emanation was the principle of "friendly persuasion," as the title of a Gary Cooper movie had it. And the moral of this tale has to do with "character building."

Once a week, on Thursdays, all students had to gather in pseudo-Gothic Clothier Memorial Hall for an hour of spiritual improvement (not necessarily of the religious kind) called Collection. The assembly was scheduled for 10 o'clock in the morning, which was not a good time after yet another night at the typewriter. But it was a good occasion for making value choices—the first step in a moral education.

Being practical folks who understood that human existence always teeters between crass self-interest and more lofty impulses, Swarthmore's Quaker-minded administration had decreed four "freebies" per semester: no retribution for resisting early-morning edification on four Thursdays of your choice. But if you chose self-indulgence (i.e., an additional hour of blissful sleep, for the fifth or *n*th time) "friendly persuasion" would set in. The wayward were not dragged from their dreams (as they might be by loud bells in a Jesuit college) but were given a choice: Pick one hour's worth of immediate gratification now, and pay with two hours of community work (in the garden or the library) at the end of the semester.

Economists call such a trade-off "present gains vs. future costs." Moralists use other terms: "choice among competing values," or "short-term vs. long-term interest," or "self vs. community." The point of this tale is not a crude utilitarian calculus, let alone goodness by imposition, but freedom tempered by rules freely accepted, if also with a little Quaker touch. Is there a better way to teach autonomous judgment to the young who have just escaped from the strictures of their parents?

To return to the beginning: For this escapee from Cold War Berlin, Swarthmore was a wondrous bildungsroman—less haphazard than Sterne's *Tristam Shandy* but more fun than Goethe's *Wilhelm Meister*—that recorded the growth of mind, soul, and character. (Or thus he believes after almost 40 years of fondest-memory mongering.) Since then, he has studied and taught at various European universities, faceless institutions that share only a faint family resemblance with the centers of distinction that Göttingen, Bologna, or Prague's Charles University once were. This experience has left him with a modest wish: May the liberal arts college, which never sank roots in continental Europe, flourish and endure. And may Swarthmore live on as its most excellent exemplar in an age when America's great research universities keep taking an ever-larger bite out of the world's intellectual and educational resources. But even at relentlessly expanding Harvard, where this student received a Ph.D., they know about excellence when they see it. They call Swarthmore "None"—as in: "Harvard Is Second to None."

⚜

Josef Joffe is the publisher and editor of the weekly newspaper Die Zeit *(Hamburg, Germany) and an associate of Harvard's Olin Institute for Strategic Studies.*

A Kind of
Holy Experiment

Dulany Ogden Bennett '66

As the head of a large independent school in the Pacific Northwest, one of my greatest goals is to nurture in the students and teachers in my care the values and perspectives that I developed at Swarthmore. William Penn called Pennsylvania his "Holy Experiment." I have always thought of Swarthmore as a kind of holy experiment in intellectual and moral community. It is that concept that I have most wanted to develop in the communities that I have served during the past 35 years, including the Oregon Episcopal School, which I now lead.

When I arrived at Swarthmore, I began to develop fearlessness about asking and answering startling questions. The courage to challenge for the sake of more closely approaching the truth was developed in me from all sides. The quality of fearless questioning marked my classes in the early years, as well as seminars in the upper-level classes. In large part, it infected me through the delightful but persistent questioning of all things philosophical and personal in my life by my roommate of four years, Janet Nordgren Stavnezer '66, who moved me to think and rethink many things in my life, as her professors and friends led her to rethink her own.

I found, at the College, not only professors but also fellow students with startling talents. A freshman math student, for instance, took over my Theoretical Calculus class when the professor was snowed in and taught the material I was struggling with as if he were a professor himself. I was so overcome with interest and curiosity, and amazed by the combination of brilliance and humility he displayed, that I found myself forgetting to feel awe and insecurity and instead fearlessly questioning him in the interest of academic passion. By the middle of freshman year, I had come to see all around me—in my fellow varsity hockey halfbacks, my dinner companions, my Saturday night dates, my fellow students, and all my professors—personal tutors and advisers, intellectual sparring partners, and potential fonts of wisdom. For me, it was like arriving on the Big Rock Candy Mountain and never getting too full.

I came to intellectual and moral maturity at Swarthmore when the Vietnam War was raging. It was a time of powerful debate that engaged us all at the intellectual and emotional levels. My male friends struggled with their decisions about graduate school, their draft registration status, and their philosophical positions about the war. Watching my friends divide along ideological lines and struggle to determine whether College friendships could survive philosophical differences made me ponder the nature of community. Over my Swarthmore career, I came to understand the power of the values of the Swarthmore community to transcend the particular differences that divided us. Even then, I could see that the kind of discourse in which class discussion—and, more powerfully, the seminar format—taught us to excel, and could teach us the civility and respect to admire each other for the integrity of our beliefs. We also developed the courage to support each other in very different life choices without having to renounce each other for our differences in values. The willingness to be fearless in our honesty yet respectful of each

At Swarthmore, I learned that a life that marries the intellectual and the moral is a productive and satisfying one.

other's integrity and intelligence created a complex and powerful sense of community: elastic, expandable, and extremely strong.

It was at Swarthmore that I first began my involvement with the American Friends Service Committee, as a member of its College Committee, helping to develop programs for male college students who were facing choices regarding the draft, and organizing peaceful protests against the war in Vietnam. I had honed my analytical skills in seminars and greatly benefited from the quality of the dialogue on campus regarding the philosophical issues surrounding the students who were facing choices about the draft. It was on this AFSC Committee that I first realized that I could be fearless in giving my opinions in the presence of strangers who were older, more experienced, and more authoritative, even when they were attempting in some subtle—and not so subtle—ways to be intimidating to younger, more inexperienced members. My Swarthmore experience had taught me to go for the truth, value my thoughts and opinions, allow myself to endure the critical feedback when I was wrong, and learn and grow from the experience. It was much more rewarding than holding back, never knowing how my views would fare in the common discourse, what they might add, or how they might further the light of truth.

As I moved on in my AFSC work to leadership roles, I realized that I benefited from lessons learned at Swarthmore that have taken longer for me to understand and acknowledge. As clerk of the AFSC board, in particular, I had to find the courage and strength within myself to silence my own opinions and preferences, and to listen for the wisdom and truth forthcoming from those gathered on the board. Deliberating in Quaker fashion, we had to discover, through the gathered wisdom, how best to deploy our human and financial resources on behalf of peace and justice in programs around the world. The stakes were high, passions were high, and the clerk needed to ensure that she could listen well in order to create a space for the authentic voices of all present to be heard. In the Quaker context, one may listen for God's leadings, but if fear, emotion, or insecurity is allowed to block the Inner Voice, or external authority or pressure to silence the authentic voice, Truth will not be heard. Thus, clear thinking, fearless speaking, and the authentic voices of all who are in possession of truth must be heard for decisions to be made that further the causes of peace and justice. I now was in a position in which I had to nurture and promote the fearlessness in the AFSC board setting that had been nurtured in me at Swarthmore.

What I have carried with me since my college days is the profound importance of linking the moral and the intellectual. Growing up as a Quaker, I was steeped in the moral values that underlie the principles on which the College rests, but too often as a child the values were presented to me in emotional and ideological terms that made them difficult for me to question or accept. Since college, I have often encountered intellectuals who have not put their academic achievements in the service of ethical pursuits. At Swarthmore, I learned that a life that marries the intellectual and the moral is a productive and satisfying one. All around me were role models of such lives, in my professors and the alumni that I knew. In my classes and seminars, and the opportunities for community service that I had, I learned how to pursue such a life.

For me, this marriage has led to a life in education and leadership. I find I have a strong preference for helping others find their paths, for maintaining balance in institutions, for leading schools that help children learn to think clearly and develop communities dedicated to service as well as learning. I am committed to schools that emphasize spiritual development and education of the whole child—spirit, mind, and body. Self-awareness, balance, and seeking the truth are themes, developed for me at Swarthmore, that thread throughout my life, both professional and personal.

For 25 years, I worked in Friends education in the greater Philadelphia area, as teacher, coach, division head, and head of school. During these years, I faced several challenges in which I had to stand alone, using the reservoir of fearlessness I had developed since my Swarthmore days. Although it was painful, to be sure, it was not difficult. There is no turning back from a conviction that becomes one's own. Moreover, the world can see both the power of that conviction and the price one is willing to pay. If you are lucky, as I ultimately was, you can bring reason to your cause, and prevail.

After taking a break to earn a doctorate in clinical psychology, in 1998 I became the head of Oregon Episcopal School. Now, I feel most successful when that sense of fearlessness or the startling truth comes bravely from a kindergarten child or a new middle school teacher, unafraid to challenge the received wisdom or the popular cause. The more frequently discourse involves engaged disagreement, close listening, and thoughtful debate, the deeper and more connected our community becomes. If our community naturally gives rise to the authentic voices of all our constituents, even those in the positions of least institutional power or those voicing the least popular positions, we will have begun to succeed. I learned to be fearless at Swarthmore. It is my hope that our students can learn fearlessness along with the kindergarten curriculum. If they do, I will chalk my contribution up to what I was so generously given by so many at Swarthmore.

Dulany Bennett, former clerk of the American Friends Service Committee, is the head of the Oregon Episcopal School in Portland.

That Exhilarating
Sense of "Aha!"

Elizabeth "Lee" Smith Ingram '66

The meaning of Swarthmore began for me when I was 9 years old and my father became president of the College. I spent my childhood in the president's house on the edge of the campus. I spent my childhood and teenage years attending wonderful choral and orchestral concerts, student plays, and the Hamburg Show in Clothier Memorial Hall. On Sunday mornings, I walked with my family to the Friends Meetinghouse and was always amazed at the number of College students who joined us there for worship. Often I returned on Sunday evenings to a packed meetinghouse to hear a speaker or panel discussion sponsored by the College on some controversial or interesting topic. I never tired of the beautiful campus with the Crum Woods, rose garden, arboretum, and especially the smell of lilacs in the springtime. In my senior year in high school, I went on a blind date with a Swarthmore freshman who ended up being my husband of 36 years (at this writing).

Applying to Swarthmore as a senior in high school was a natural progression for me. I remember having an interview with Bob Barr '56, the dean of admissions, and coming out of it convinced more than ever that this was the place for me. I might add parenthetically that my husband, my son, and almost everyone else I know who was interviewed by Bob Barr ended up making the College his or her first choice! Alas, my family persuaded me to go elsewhere my freshman year, so I set off north to college. Fortunately, I was able to return to Swarthmore my sophomore year, and, I must admit, it truly felt like coming home.

Being a student at Swarthmore was like being a child in a candy store: so many rich choices of courses and areas of study. I remember sitting on the edge of my seat in classes where such professors as Hedley Rhys introduced art history or Tom Blackburn and Harold Pagliaro conveyed the excitement of English literature. Choosing a major at Swarthmore proved to be a precursor to choosing a career—you try out different areas until you find the major or career that is the best intersection between what you are good at and what you like to do. I settled on English literature.

Majoring in English and taking an education course with Alice Brodhead played a big part in my career choice. In typical Swarthmore fashion, Professor Brodhead fired her students up about the issues, needs, and challenges of elementary and secondary education, then sent us into the neighboring classrooms to give it a try. I was assigned to Swarthmore High School to teach *The Merchant of Venice* to a 10th-grade honors class. To the horror of Professor Sam Hynes' daughter, who happened to be in the class and recognized me as one of her neighbors, the teacher handed the whole unit and class over to me and left the room. That's how my teaching career was launched. Here, and in other classrooms in England, Massachusetts, and D.C., I experienced the thrill and satisfaction of taking a piece of literature I had studied and using it to spark discussions and excite students about literature in the same way that Swarthmore professors had inspired me.

I describe myself as an educator at this point because my career has gone in several directions, with education the unifying theme. Besides teaching English literature, I have trained teachers, been an adjunct professor at a university, coordinated programs, and worked as an educational researcher and consultant. In addition, in my search for a professional niche where I could work part time while raising three children, I discovered the world of educational diagnosis and have spent many years helping children and adults understand why learning is difficult for them and how they can overcome their learning challenges. Again, I feel a gratitude for my Swarthmore education as an English major. The same skills that were brought to bear in analyzing a poem or a novel—the piecing together of clues of character, setting, and plot that led to the full understanding of the theme of the piece of literature—have been transferable to analyzing the clues and patterns that shed light on an individual's learning disability. And there is that same exhilarating sense of "Aha!" when the pieces seem to fall into place and reveal the whole.

Swarthmore also taught me another important lesson: that balance in life matters even when work is a priority. Sports was my outlet, and I have fond memories of playing hockey and lacrosse all of my years at Swarthmore. Our coach, Pete Hess, projected such a healthy attitude about the place of athletics at Swarthmore. Under her guidance, we practiced rigorously, played our games with spirit and a keen desire to win, but always knew that she would understand if an important science lab or exam became the higher priority. Years later, in my 40s, I joined a women's soccer team, complete with official uniforms, referees, and even yellow cards for misbehavior. As we practiced and played our games, running around outdoors on a beautiful fall or spring day, memories came flooding back to me of my Swarthmore days and the wonderful feeling of camaraderie and well-being that playing on a sports team brings.

But Swarthmore has never been just about ourselves. The campus culture always encouraged the use of one's education

The campus culture always encouraged the use of one's education to make the world a better place.

to make the world a better place. As the country struggled with issues of civil rights and social justice, we students tried to do our own bit. I remember vividly the excitement and satisfaction when a group of us participated in the College's first Upward Bound Program in the summer after my sophomore year. Our job was to teach a group of Chester students math, English, drama, and other subjects in ways that would give them a taste of the excitement of learning and help motivate them to higher achievement. Then, during the year, we tutored many of these students. I think this experience set the stage for my community activities. As a PTA leader and activist in my children's schools and in our county school system, I grappled with the issues of how to improve the educational opportunities and success rate of children who come from disadvantaged backgrounds. My work in these areas led to my Ph.D. dissertation topic, which concerned the ways to increase enrollment in honors and Advanced Placement classes of African American and Hispanic students.

However, no discussion of the meaning of Swarthmore would be complete without reference to the wonderful people who were fellow students or with whom I had contact later as alums. I remember the lively and thought-provoking discussions in the dining hall or in the dorms, and the whimsical and humorous moments, such as the "Midnight Mile" run around the track behind the Lamb-Miller Field House (which, I confess, I watched appreciatively rather than ran) and the time during the Centennial Fund Campaign when *The Phoenix* announced on April 1 that the president had inadvertently sold the College to the Ford Foundation. Many of the friendships begun there have endured and enriched my life. At reunions, as our class moves closer and closer to the front of the alumni parade, I realize how our common Swarthmore experience bonds us together in very meaningful ways. Sometimes in my community, while serving on a task force or on the board of a school, I unexpectedly find another Swarthmore graduate in the room; or I find that another alum is a member of my Friends Meeting; or I discover a fellow Swarthmorean running for Congress, as was the case in this past election. It is always a pleasant surprise when this happens because I realize that I am working or interacting with another like-minded person who shares Swarthmore's values of being open to new ideas, reasoning a problem through in a creative way, and seeking action to ameliorate societal problems that we care deeply about.

Perhaps the truest meaning of Swarthmore was captured, however, when my oldest child decided to attend the College. When my husband and I helped him move into his Wharton dormitory room, we were surprised at how excited we both felt. Part of our excitement stemmed from the realization that we would gain yet another excuse to visit the beautiful campus, hear firsthand about Swarthmore events and issues, and come to know a new generation of Swarthmore students. But most important, we realized that our son was going to continue the Swarthmore tradition for our family and have the same chance that we were given to spend undergraduate years at this truly extraordinary college.

⁂

Lee Ingram is an educational diagnostician, researcher, and consultant based in Washington, D.C.

Back to Community

Sam Newbury '67

W hen I first started work for Fred Rogers' production company, I was surprised to learn that *Mister Rogers' Neighborhood* generated a small but consistent stream of correspondence from college students even though its intended audience was preschoolers. I asked the program's consultant, Dr. Margaret McFarland, why this was happening, and she replied that it made perfect sense. "You see, going away to college is all about the same issues that occupy preschoolers—autonomy and separation. Preschoolers are struggling to separate themselves from almost absolute dependence on their parents and to understand themselves as separate and unique individuals. They are moving outside the small orbit of home into a wider world." Then it was easy to see how the process was being repeated on a larger scale with the move to college. Thinking of Dr. McFarland and her deep understanding of children reminds me of another saying she often quoted: "Character is caught, not taught." If we learn from the models around us far better than the lessons taught us, then the values and culture of that wider world into which we enter during important times of transition have a significant impact.

I had grown up and gone to school in a suburb of Boston. Concord, Mass., had a great history and high standards for education, although in the 1950s it was more a suburb than an independent town. It had lost some of its economic diversity while holding onto its dominant mainstream culture of New England Protestantism. When the time came to think about colleges, the only real qualification for me was to be outside of New England. I must have felt that some geographical separation would help me gain a chance to define myself. Swarthmore, with its location in Pennsylvania, qualified. But I wonder whether a sense of the Quaker heritage wasn't also a factor. I'd been to several college interviews, all pretty standard, but when we stopped at Swarthmore, the interviewer didn't ask for my list of accomplishments. Instead, he opened a discussion on my impressions of my private-school secondary education. He listened, and probed my answers. I came away very impressed, and it was a first taste of some important things about Swarthmore.

What that interview showed me was a keen interest in ideas and open discussion, a respect for an individual's thoughtful opinions, and an embrace of the possibility of learning something new. I felt engaged as an individual with something to offer and invited to enter into the give-and-take of learning. It quickly became the basis for my decision to make Swarthmore my first choice.

When I arrived on campus in 1963 in the middle of the Chester civil rights actions, it was quickly apparent that people were expected to consider seriously the issues of society and to take action, if that was what they thought appropriate. Many classmates seemed far ahead of me in this; my classmate John Lewis was arrested one day in Chester, and I had to substitute for him on very short notice in a production of *Death of a Salesman*. Acting in that role was the beginning of what would turn out to be a major part of my life at Swarthmore, although it was also a lesson to me that John had done some-

The respect for each individual's capacity to consider and decide went very deep and infused much of what happened at college.

thing I hadn't even considered. It was an early introduction to the Quaker tradition of taking responsibility for oneself and one's actions.

But there was also apparent in the civil rights demonstrations, and the reaction to the Vietnam War soon to come, a sense that this was serious business. Decisions deserved a thorough investigation and thoughtful consideration. Also interwoven was a strong sense that different individuals might come to different decisions, based on their own experience and conscience. This was heady stuff for someone breaking away from the haven of childhood and family. To me, it felt deeply based in the environment of faith and intellectual rigor that informed the Quakers. The respect for each individual's capacity to consider and decide went very deep and, I believe, infused much of what happened at college, whether formally or informally. I'm sure I didn't always succeed in emulating this, but it was a goal, and it was mourned when I ignored it in the exuberance of being freed of childhood restrictions or when the desire to conform overcame a commitment to decide for myself. The environment of this new, wider world was surely shaping me. Some important values were being "caught."

The forums and "teach-ins" about the Vietnam War also contained within them a basic optimism about the impact of knowledge and the importance of engagement in the community. Again, it seemed part and parcel of the Quaker tradition, which militated against cynicism and hopelessness. All of this was part of a love of learning—and a deep respect for what it could offer—that was very much a part of many academic courses at Swarthmore, too. Now, in my 50s, I've found a chance to return to being a part-time university student. The delight and excitement of learning, awakened at Swarthmore, are still very much alive.

However, it is that other element of the College community's reaction to the war for which I am most grateful. The sense of responsibility for being engaged with one's own community and the wish to make it better—more just, more compassionate, more open to a wide range of people and ideas— leads me now. With the underlying optimism, tempered with the acknowledgment that change takes time, it has been a powerful goal toward which to strive.

Looking back, Swarthmore not only helped me to define myself and to see myself as capable and responsible, but it turned me back toward community. Knowledge, as attractive as it is, is in the service of the larger group—a whole "neighborhood" of people who live together and care for one another. I remain profoundly grateful that I was given the opportunity to leave the tunnel of self-absorption that so often characterized my adolescence and discover myself at Swarthmore.

༄

Sam Newbury was the producer of the PBS children's television series
Mr. Rogers' Neighborhood.

Humble
Arrogance

John Mather '68

To me, Swarthmore was my first chance to meet a lot of people like myself, to make new friends, and to test whether I was capable of achieving my dreams in the Big World. My childhood stories were of Galileo and Darwin and Newton and Einstein, and I wanted to understand how the universe really works. I had the bravery of one who has not yet been tested. But at Swarthmore, I met people—friends and faculty—for whom such dreams were the normal, if unexpressed, way of life.

Of course, we would learn calculus and chemistry and astronomy and physics. Of course, we would think about relativity and the weird nature of space and time. Of course, we would wonder how particles of matter could be waves described by complex numbers. Downstairs in the basement of DuPont, we measured the force of gravity really precisely; we measured the speed of light; we made some electronic circuits; and we measured nuclear magnetic resonance the old way, with magnets and surplus microwave hardware (before the technique became a medical standard). And from there, we would go on to the *really* hard puzzles, of science and of more complex things not yet approached by science.

Nature's final exams are a lot less organized than a college course—and unforgiving as well.

I chose Swarthmore over Harvard, MIT, Caltech, and Princeton, partly because it had a well-organized physics program that covered everything neatly and partly for the nice feel of the campus. I was a little intimidated by the Big City, and I liked the quiet of the College. I had grown up in rural New Jersey on the Rutgers Agricultural Experiment Station, where my father was a scientist studying dairy cattle, but it was way out in the country, and school was an hour's ride away on the bus. Swarthmore was a good place to study, and it was respectable to be a nerd, before the term was coined.

So, how did it all turn out? Just fine. From Swarthmore, I went on to Berkeley and got into measuring the spectrum of the cosmic microwave background radiation. It is the very faint echo of the Big Bang itself; at the time, we could barely detect it. It had just been discovered in 1965, just up the road in New Jersey, while I was still a Swarthmore student. Nevertheless, our business was to have the chutzpah to try to measure it much better than ever before, using a balloon to carry a payload above the interference of the Earth's atmosphere. Previously, as a Swarthmore student, I had been enjoying the challenge and thought maybe by hard work I'd learn a lot, and then exams came, and I felt the excitement of being able to figure things out. But now, I was getting the feeling that doing science was to be always up against the unknown and the unknowable; it was a rare day when I really felt I knew what I was doing. Indeed, the first flight of the balloon payload was a failure for three different reasons. Nature's final exams are a lot less organized than a college course—and unforgiving as well.

I went on from there to keep on whacking away at impossible problems. I went to work for NASA and organized a team to build the Cosmic Background Explorer (COBE) satellite to measure the cosmic background radiation better, and I came to appreciate how much modern science is a team sport. We advanced the state of the art by orders of magnitude; made the front pages of the news around the world; and made a book of our story, *The Very First Light*. The topic is still hot, and my colleagues have found ways to learn about the fundamental forces that move the universe by examining the radiation in even more detail. Now, I've moved to another project, to build the James Webb Space Telescope to follow after the famous Hubble Space Telescope, and it seems even more difficult and more important than the COBE.

Now that I've worked as a professional scientist for a few decades, I feel just as ignorant as I did when I walked into Swarthmore, and I still have the nerve to try to unlock the secrets. It takes an odd sort of humble arrogance to even attempt to do this. I have a deep sense of the mystery of nature, and I'm constantly amazed at how much we've learned as puny humans, but there are billions of us, crawling all over everything like ants, bringing back our treasures, telling our friends, and putting our discoveries in the libraries of paper and electrons. There's a kind of immortality about writing things down for the world to see.

⚶

John Mather, senior astrophysicist at NASA's Goddard Space Flight Center, is working on the development of the James Webb Space Telescope, which will replace the Hubble Space Telescope.

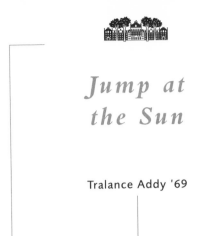

Jump at the Sun

Tralance Addy '69

I had been in the United States for three weeks when freshman orientation at Swarthmore started in the fall of 1965. Almost everything around me was new, and I was excited about my new surroundings, which clearly were dramatically different from my home in Ghana. While I knew that leaving Ghana to come to Swarthmore would make an important difference in my life, I could not, in those early days, separate the specific role of Swarthmore from the general impact of the experiences I was having as a newcomer to the United States or, for that matter, the novelty of college life for a typical student on any campus. The distinctive influence of Swarthmore only started to get untangled from that general American experience long after I had left Swarthmore, and it has happened over the years in fits and bursts, as I reflect from time to time on the motivations and influences for what I have chosen to do with my life and how I have gone about it.

In sorting out the role of Swarthmore in my personal and professional growth, I have found it helpful to recall some important events and turning points—some exhilarating, and some painful. To begin with, Swarthmore is, after all, the place of my first real introduction to America, bringing the America I observed on campus into confrontation with my views of America shaped by years of Hollywood movies and propaganda from U.S. government publications exported to developing countries around the world. It is the place where, for the first time, I discovered, during an introductory philosophy course taught by Hans Oberdiek, that what I thought and had to say was not only distinctive but of interest to others, and worthy of serious consideration. It is the place where I made the liberating discovery that while I had a lot to learn, I also had something worthwhile to contribute to the community. It is the place where, through humanities courses I never would have had the chance to take in Ghana, I came to realize that simply pursuing my interests in science and engineering was not going to be sufficient for me.

It is also the place where I was assailed by feelings of guilt about not doing enough. When it was announced upon my graduation that I was the first in the College's history to graduate with two separate degrees within four years, my pride was mixed with guilt, because I knew I could have done better.

Swarthmore was also the place where I was first introduced to student political action, and the strong sense that the best academic training had very little meaning without social conscience. It was a place of unceasing intellectual discussion in pursuit of meaning, seemingly about *everything*! It was the place where, I can say now quite comfortably, I met some of the most principled people that I have encountered in my life, including both faculty and students. It was the place where I got to see up close a unique face of America, full of unapologetic idealism and passion about morality, integrity, and social justice that were to become important parts of the barometer for my own journey through life, often in environments where such concerns have seemed in short supply.

I entered Swarthmore as a somewhat idealistic student

Fulfillment for me has been highest when trying to address important and unaddressed issues, often associated with a high risk of failure.

with an image of myself as someone who enjoyed marching to a different drummer. I was to learn very quickly that, in fact, Swarthmore was a breeding ground for nonconformists, and that students and faculty alike prided themselves on being driven by forces different from what motivated most of their counterparts in the country. While it robbed me of some of the pleasure of thinking myself a nonconformist, being in a place where everyone else seemed to be one paid me back by reinforcing the notion that standing on one's individual beliefs, regardless of popular or accepted norms, is something to be cherished and respected. Years later, my wife commented that she could often tell who were the likely Swarthmore alumni in any group by looking for the people with the most unusual personal and career involvements.

At the age of 14, I had joined a relatively small group of secondary school student volunteers of the Voluntary Work Camps Association of Ghana, through which we spent weekends and long vacations in villages and rural towns, building schools, roads, community centers, and sometimes public latrines. I immensely enjoyed my time in these villages, and I include among my proudest accomplishments in life the small contributions I made as an apprentice brick mason and enthusiastic volunteer, to help make a difference. Later, I was to discover that such involvement was, in fact, the norm for Swarthmore students and alumni.

Looking back, I have marveled at how so many impressive human beings could be in, or associated with, such a relatively small college. In my "space," for example, there was Betz Morrill, an engineering professor who showed uncommon interest, understanding, and support for me and other international students, and who helped me understand that engineering was a tool that could be used to achieve higher goals of service to society. Early in my life at Swarthmore, I also met Carl and Bunty Barus, two remarkable people whose example of dedication to building a better world, and principled opposition to injustice everywhere, I have held up as an ideal from my student days to the very present. Carl was also an engineering professor and, although I took only one course that he taught, I had the unusual opportunity to develop what for me was one of the most important and lasting friendships I have had in America, a friendship through which I examined many of my important choices and actions.

As I was to find out after I left Swarthmore, the intimate and passionate involvement of engineering faculty and students in social and political action was not the norm outside the campus. Clearly, Swarthmore engineers were "wired" differently.

In trying to understand Swarthmore's influence on how I am wired, I have often thought about one particular incident. I do not recall the exact details, but for the semester finals of one course we had been given a take-home three-hour exam. As I looked through the exam, I noticed that the last question stated, simply, "Ask yourself a question, and answer it." I badly needed to get a good grade on the exam, but for some reason I spent most of the allotted time in an effort to craft the most elegant and important question I could think of. Needless to say, the question was so elegant, I was not able to answer it. I have continued to wonder why I had not focused on the grade I needed, instead of on the importance of the question. I am still waiting for the answer, but as some would say, it was a very Swarthmore kind of act—perhaps a little short on pragmatism, but definitely long on idealism. I can now say, however, that the habit and sense of comfort I gained from posing important and difficult questions to myself have been instrumental to my personal and professional growth.

In retrospect, with some diversions here and there, my personal and professional paths seem to have been filled unconsciously with a string of unconventional choices, and fulfillment for me has been highest when trying to address important and unaddressed issues, often associated with a high risk of failure. Somehow, the fascination with the big questions, and the potential to make an important difference in tackling them, make the risks look a little smaller, or at least worth taking.

After Swarthmore I started graduate school in mechanical and aerospace engineering. However, it was 1969, and feeling a need for my work to be relevant to the issues of the time, I developed a strong interest in the problem of world hunger, and subsequently switched fields to food engineering, eventually writing a doctoral thesis on the direct conversion of protein from unconventional sources, as a way of addressing the protein deficiency suffered by much of the world's population. My first real paying job was as a research engineer at Scott Paper Co., where I joined a small group of engineers in an effort to produce paper through an unconventional and, at the time, novel technology that holds promise for relatively poor nations with limited resources to make certain types of paper products with minimal environmental impact. Although the project was largely successful, I gradually found some difficulty in relating the development of softer toilet tissue to the great social and economic issues that needed to be addressed.

I ended up switching careers to become involved in health care, accepting a position at Johnson & Johnson. During 20 years that I consider to be some of the most productive and fulfilling of my life, I had the good fortune to lead the development of important technologies, to start new ventures, and to build companies around the world. In fact, it was a career that went beyond my initial expectations. Nevertheless, there were still the nagging questions. Was I doing enough? Should my life have greater meaning outside corporate America? Was I too comfortable? My eventual decision was that I could do more of what was emotionally important to me, and two years ago I became the founder of Plebys International, a new company with a mission to develop technology-based enterprises that address critical needs among the 80 percent of the world's population with little access to most products and services found in the highly developed nations. It is a largely uncharted path, but the emotional benefits are high. As, I am told, the old African proverb goes: "Never hesitate to jump at the sun. It doesn't matter if you reach the sun, but at least your feet will have left the earth."

Would I have traveled this road without going through Swarthmore? It is possible. What I do know is that the experiences and influences I gained during those years have been excellent components of my personal compass, and, as a result, the choices and commitments have been easier to make.

Tralance Addy is the founder and president of Plebys International, a worldwide technology-based enterprise development company.

A Quality
of Kindness

Nancy Bekavac '69

The day after my father died, Saturday, Feb. 27, 1965, I received a telegram from Swarthmore College. It began, "We are delighted. . . ." I can still see those words on the pale yellow paper because, at that time and in that place—my father's office—I could not imagine how those words could possibly apply.

The telegram was an invitation to Swarthmore College to be interviewed for a White Open Scholarship. The interviews would be held the next weekend, and I was invited to come on Friday. As I was reading the telegram, my mother came in and asked what it was. "It's Swarthmore," I said. "They want me to come and interview for a scholarship next weekend." She asked me what I wanted to do. "I think I'll go," I said. She agreed, and then we went to my father's wake.

My father was buried that Monday. My uncle Ken offered to drive me to Swarthmore on Thursday, an all-day drive from our home just outside Pittsburgh. On Friday morning, it started to rain, and I arrived at Swarthmore in a drizzle. I remember the way the wet gray stone glistened and how the rhododendrons around Worth looked. I was met by a friendly student guide named Elenor ("Call me Muffin") Reid '67, who grabbed my suitcase and started showing me around even before my uncle's car had pulled away. I was a slightly numbed version of the real me.

I remember meeting other Swarthmore students and then being ushered into Bond. I met some of the other candidates—Ken Roberts, Christine Grant, Marilyn Holifield—and then a very tall, thin man with dark hair and a large smile took center stage. He seemed to know each of us. He pronounced my name correctly (a rare occurrence), and I remember asking him if he was the basketball coach.

"I'm Fred Hargadon," he said. "I'm the dean of admissions." I knew I had committed a *faux pas* (not a phrase I could have pronounced at the time, although it was a concept with which I was intimately familiar), but he seemed unconcerned by my ignorance. He congratulated us on having been selected for the competition, and then he told us that we had all been admitted to Swarthmore College. A committee would interview each of us during the next day or so, and we would be free to leave on Sunday. Soon afterward, he assured us, we would be told what the committee had decided.

It was then, I think, that Dean Hargadon explained that the scholarship included room and board as well as full tuition. I know that he said the scholarship was not based on need, so there was no financial-aid form required. That jolted me a little. Only two weeks before, I had had my first and only discussion with my father about financing my college education—the Saturday before he died. We sat down, and he explained to me—for the first time—how much he made, what he had saved, and how we could afford college for me even while my brother was at Notre Dame. My father told me that he could afford tuition wherever I wanted to go, and he would not fill out a financial-aid form.

The discussion in Bond with Dean Hargadon had come uncomfortably close to what I was very busy trying not to think about. I was blinking back tears and fiddling with a teacup to cover up my discomfort. Luckily, we then all got up to go to dinner.

I have a series of pictures in my head from that weekend: a class on American intellectual history with Professor Robert Bannister; he was lecturing on Louis Sullivan's buildings in Chicago. I wanted never to leave—and I promptly decided to major in history. Someone walked me down to the Crum, and somehow, I met up with the only other Clairton High School student to go to Swarthmore, Joyce Milton '67. She was a junior, and her mother was our town librarian.

I remember being struck by a quality of kindness in the way I was treated by everyone—not by just the women but the male students and staff, too. I told some about my father's death, usually because I couldn't avoid it. Some asked me if I wanted to be alone; some were just silent and nodded. Both reactions helped me get through the weekend.

Of all the memories of that weekend, the clearest are of my interview. There was a committee of two faculty members and two students, as I recall, in the semidark of one of the lodges. One of the professors sat far back in a large wing chair, and the committee formed a little half circle around the candidate. The questions were wonderful—clearly, they had read my folder carefully. The wing-chair professor asked one of the first questions: "Who is your favorite poet?" I thought a minute and said, "Rudyard Kipling." He quickly blurted out, "What about him?"

"The rhyme schemes, the meter," I replied and started quoting something like *Danny Deaver*. He waved his hands to indicate "Enough," and we wandered on to other topics— writing, biochemistry, astronomy, and politics. Near the end, the same professor tried again. "Other than Mr. Kipling, is there any other poet you like?" There was more than a tinge of sarcasm.

"I could say Shakespeare," I said, "but that's like saying you like English poetry. I suppose you expect me to say T.S. Eliot,

> *I was blinking back tears and fiddling with a teacup to cover up my discomfort.*

but there is someone I've just read who I think is better than Kipling and better than Eliot by far, but I don't know much about him. His name is W.B. Yeats." I pronounced it "Yeets."

"Oh, yes, Yeats," the professor said, using my mispronunciation. "What poems?" "'Speech After Long Silence' is one, and 'The Choice' is another," I said, trying to sound as though I had some critical basis for these judgments.

"Oh, fine," he said, and settled back into his chair. That was how I first met Samuel Hynes.

The next day, my uncle picked me up on schedule, and we drove straight back across Pennsylvania. When we got home, Mom asked me about the weekend, and I told her how kind everyone had been. I also spoke with my favorite English teacher and told her about the interview. She grabbed my hand. "Oh, Nancy," she said in her soft voice. "It's pronounced 'Yates'." Then I told her how the professor had repeated my pronunciation, and I realized what he'd done for me. A correction, however kind, would have cracked the veneer of my self-confidence.

The following day, I received a letter from Swarthmore telling me I had been awarded the scholarship. But that was not what reduced me to tears. There was a warm note from Dean Hargadon, expressing his sympathy on my father's death. I realized from his letter that he had known all that weekend and had had the grace and judgment to say nothing, to let me feel my own way through my visit. He wrote that the committee had not been informed about my father's death until after they had made their recommendations. That meant that I was judged more or less on my own merits and that the scholarship was not a kind of consolation prize for losing my father.

In my junior year at Swarthmore, in the spring of 1968, in one of those magical educational moments that alumni remember all their lives, four of us in a seminar in moral philosophy found in Immanuel Kant's work a set of principles and a way of reasoning that grounded ethics in the radical notion that each intelligent being owed recognition to the interests of other intelligent beings. The philosophy of Swarthmore—the Quaker notion that recognizes in each human being the capacity to bring a singular "light" to bear in the world—parallels Kant's precepts, at least in requiring respect for others' interests.

Very often, the most intense intellectual life is characterized as being removed from common concerns, from "mere" human sympathy and small, sentimental gestures of interest, pity, or politeness. That has never seemed to me the way real intellectual depth is reflected in life. Here, I hold with Kant that disinterested reason requires respect for others, and the value we set on our own humanity is reflected in the way we treat others.

After Swarthmore, I paid great attention to the quality of the discussions and relationships I had with those at the law school I attended, with the judge I clerked for, and at the law firm I joined. I kept Swarthmore's philosophy in mind when I left the law firm to work for a foundation, then for a reforming president of Dartmouth College, and then to become president of Scripps College. Looking at these choices, I see that I have almost always chosen small institutions characterized by intellectual intensity and a sense of civic, communal obligation—institutions where the influence of one person can make a difference, where I believed that ethics played a critical role in decisions.

I will never forget my first weekend at Swarthmore and the kindness shown to a silently grieving, naive young woman. I cannot claim that I have lived out in my life the examples of the many kindnesses I received at Swarthmore, or that I have lived up to the principles of Kant as we discussed them in 1968 and after. But I have tried to bring to my work as a lawyer, a foundation executive, and a college administrator the principle of recognizing the humanity of others through my actions.

※

Nancy Bekavac is the president of Scripps College.

Tradition
Amid Change

Mary Schmidt Campbell '69

When I came to Swarthmore College in the fall of 1965, American colleges and universities—Swarthmore among them—were experiencing a crisis of conscience. Admissions policies at many of the country's most elite colleges restricted the number of black students admitted, no matter how stellar their academic credentials. In true Swarthmore fashion, the College, under the leadership of then President Courtney Smith and Dean of Admissions Fred Hargadon, decided to attack the issue in a definitive manner. In one sweeping action, they affirmed the College's commitment to the progressive ideals of the civil rights movement by accepting virtually every qualified black student who applied. My class, with a larger cohort of black students than ever before in the history of the College, entered Swarthmore one year after the Civil Rights Act and just months after the passage of the Voting Rights Act. We entered with experiences, histories, cultural backgrounds, and expectations new to most in the Swarthmore community. If ever there was a moment when the meaning of Swarthmore was challenged, it was with the arrival of the Class of 1969.

Swarthmore's action, in and of itself a confirmation of

many of its core values, heightened a fundamental "Swarthmore Paradox." On the one hand, encouraging heretical thinking, questioning the status quo, investigating the complexity of issues are at the heart of Swarthmore's claim on excellence. On the other hand, Swarthmore is an intensely traditional place where challenge and heresy sometimes clash with the College's sense of those deeply ingrained, enduring traditions. If change was the theme song of our class, the leitmotiv of that song was a set of fundamental questions about the role of diversity. The arrival of our class set into motion what would become an ongoing Socratic institutional inquiry. Does diversity play a role in building a student body? What is the value of a diverse community? If diversity is valuable, how does a traditional and heretofore racially homogeneous community embrace difference?

My experience during those years is instructive. Although I came from one of Philadelphia's most prestigious public high schools, the Swarthmore classroom offered as exciting an intellectual experience as I had ever encountered. We were expected to master our massive reading lists with a thoroughness and depth that required us not only to have read the texts, but to have interrogated their assumptions and penetrated their complexity, reveling in the creative clash and dissonance of competing ideas. The insights and discoveries that came from the best of my courses were nothing short of exhilarating. I felt as though I were an athlete in training. In this case, it was to develop the muscles of my intellect, to develop a habit of mind that was rigorous, disciplined, demanding, and assertive in its approach to a subject, any subject—a habit of mind that would stay with me for the rest of my life. In this arena, the meaning of Swarthmore at that time was confident and bold. Embracing cultural difference, however, was another matter.

This academic richness notwithstanding, Swarthmore's intense, insulated social culture was totally alien to me. I was

If ever there was a moment when the meaning of Swarthmore was challenged, it was with the arrival of the Class of 1969.

ready to transfer by the end of my freshman year. In an effort to keep me, one of the deans, Susan Cobbs, suggested that I commute from my home in inner-city Philadelphia, and I did. But if Swarthmore was alien to me, my urban experience was utterly alien to many of my classmates. There are any number of illustrations I could cite, but two stand out. On a trip to the Philadelphia Museum of Art, as we drove past my West Philadelphia house, one of my classmates, unaware that we were in my neighborhood, lamented, "I don't know how anyone could live here." At which point I answered, "I do." The chasm between my inner-city experience and the Swarthmore campus intensified as the civil rights movement culminated in the assassination of Dr. Martin Luther King. The morning after he was shot, my street was filled with armored tanks, and helmeted police were on the rooftops of the stores, their guns drawn, dogs by their side. By the time I arrived at Swarthmore, I was shaking. Swarthmore, on the other hand, seemed unfazed by King's death. People played Frisbee on the lawn, and classroom discussions barely acknowledged that an event of any consequence had occurred. In those days, there was little on campus that assisted in acknowledging or reconciling difference.

The unrest in my West Philadelphia neighborhood was by no means unique, and that year, 1968, the country witnessed the flare of racial tensions, as Newark, Harlem, and countless other cities and towns suffered devastating riots. It wasn't long before the country's urban unrest made its way onto college campuses. Swarthmore found itself in the pages of *Life* magazine, after a group of my classmates took over the administration building, and, in the course of the protest, President Smith suffered a fatal heart attack in his office. What did this event mean to Swarthmore and its core values? Little did I realize that when I graduated—wearing a black arm band to protest the war in Vietnam, a big afro to assert my identity, and a resolve never to come back to campus—part of the meaning of Swarthmore was that there would be an ongoing dialogue to probe that question.

What has been most remarkable in my experience is the institution's unwillingness to let me go. Like Dean Cobbs' insistence that we find a way for me to stay, the College in the past 35 years has been insistent that I—and its alumni in general—stay a part of the ongoing dialogue and dialectic that compose the discourse of the community. I have learned in the decades since I left that essential to the meaning of Swarthmore is the way in which it becomes a lifelong enterprise, a living community for its members. As an alumna, over the years, my connections to the Swarthmore community have deepened. A lecture on campus, hosting an alumni event when I was director of the Studio Museum in Harlem; serving first on the Alumni Council, then on the Board of Managers; making annual gifts; and watching my own son experience four years that could not have been more different from mine have drawn me closer to the College. In that relationship, I have witnessed the same rigor, discipline, and tough investigation of difficult issues, such as the debate on diversity, that I found in the classroom when I was a student. That demanding habit of mind has served the College well. Swarthmore is a place that allows itself and the members of its community to be reenergized and renewed by change, even as it sustains its enduring traditions.

&

Mary Schmidt Campbell, former cultural affairs commissioner of New York City, is dean of the Tisch School of the Arts at New York University.

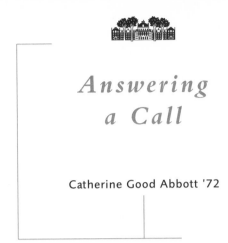

Answering a Call

Catherine Good Abbott '72

In 2003, after 27 years in the business world, I left the executive ranks of a large energy company to answer God's call to ministry. A dramatic life change? Yes—a change that had its roots in my formative experiences at Swarthmore College. Thirty-five years earlier, I entered Swarthmore planning to become a research chemist. Instead, I graduated as a religion major, believing that, for my life to have meaning, I must act to make a difference in the world. Swarthmore taught me a great deal academically and intellectually. But more important, the enduring life lessons I learned there formed me as a Christian, gave me a sense of social responsibility, and set me on a life's journey in which changing fields and domains has become a way of life. What *is* it about Swarthmore that shaped my life so dramatically?

The Religion Department faculty—Patrick Henry, Don Swearer, and Lin Urban—had a tremendous influence. Patrick invited me to join him in teaching a Wednesday-night Christian-education class for junior high students at the local Presbyterian church. I can recall Patrick speculating about what it might be like if Jesus appeared among us today—how radical his message would sound to us and how few who

Sometimes you learn the most when you are stumbling.

called themselves Christians would embrace him. I can remember Don Swearer regaling us, over a meal at his house, with stories of his failure as a Fuller Brush salesman during his graduate school years. I marveled at the humility of this admired professor of Eastern religions, making himself vulnerable to his students by telling us about the low periods in his life.

In the fall of my senior year, the department chair, Lin Urban, counseled me to drop honors. He told me that the quality of my work was not up to honors standards, that I was merely parroting what I was reading, that I was not really thinking critically and coming to my own conclusions. In retrospect, I can see that my difficulties were caused, in part, by changing domains—while I was steeped in math and the sciences, I was still unsure of myself in the humanities and did not have the courage to try out my own ideas. My reaction was anger—I would show Lin Urban how wrong he was! I redoubled my efforts and really pushed myself to think more deeply and reach conclusions—and slowly the feedback improved. I had never come so close to failure. Eventually, I did graduate with high honors, much to the pleasure of the religion faculty. Today, I owe a good deal of my ability to think critically to Lin Urban and the push he gave me (as uncomfortable as it was at the time). In recent years, Lin and I have become good friends as we have co-chaired an effort to raise an endowment for a Protestant ministry on campus.

From the religion faculty, I learned that you have to take risks in order to grow and that sometimes you learn the most when you are stumbling. These professors were people whose lives embodied their stories—professors who cared about their students as whole people, who respected us as persons (even if we were not doing well academically), and who helped us grow and develop our own visions of how to live authentic lives.

The Swarthmore years were a "coming of age" time for me, a time for developing a sense of social responsibility. The Vietnam War and the invasion of Cambodia, the occupation of the Admissions Office by African American students, and the death of our president Courtney Smith disrupted my college years (1968-1972). These painful experiences shaped me as I participated in a Swarthmore community that, in dealing seriously with these events, treated everyone with dignity, regardless of differing positions on these divisive issues. The way we struggled together with the moral and social issues persuaded me that religious convictions needed to be expressed in action in the world. These convictions led me to government service in energy policy and eventually to my current service on the boards of The Nature Conservancy and Resources for the Future.

My work in energy policy opened up an opportunity to move to Houston and work for the company that later became Enron. During the 10 years I worked for Enron, it was viewed as an innovative, fast-growing company. When I left in 1995, Enron was still much admired and was the darling of Wall Street. Early on, at Enron, I concluded that what I wanted was to become the president of a business unit. Slowly, however, I realized that I was unlikely to achieve my goal of running a company at Enron. And despite the external adulation Enron was receiving, there was something deeper that was bothering me about the company. I certainly did not anticipate the corruption and greed that led to Enron's downfall in late 2001. However, in 1992, my return to Swarthmore for my 20th reunion played a key role in my growing conviction that I needed to take a good, hard look at my life. A weekend's worth of long talks and thoughtful questions posed by my old and dear friends from Swarthmore led to a period of reexamination of my life and career goals. Was I really cut out to be a profit-and-loss corporate leader? Was Enron the right place for me? Should I return to not-for-profit work? One friend even suggested that I consider the ministry.

These questions were pushed aside when, in 1996, an opportunity arrived for me to fulfill my ambition to run a business. I was offered the presidency of Columbia Gas Transmission, the largest subsidiary of Columbia Energy Group. I accepted the long-coveted role with a sense of mission. I wanted to deliver strong results for the shareholders, but I wanted to do it in a way that committed the employees to strive not just for excellence but for excellence with a heart—a goal that, I believe, came directly from my experiences at Swarthmore. The resilience I learned at Swarthmore in my near-failure with the Honors Program served me well in corporate life. However, in late 2000, another company acquired Columbia, and, two years later, I left corporate America to begin my new journey in God's service. While I had tried, in my own imperfect way, to live a responsible and faithful life, I now heard God calling me—in a direct and forceful way—to return to school and become an ordained minister.

So how, then, did Swarthmore shape my life? Swarthmore gave me a solid foundation for my search for meaning—not always successful—in a variety of realms. Swarthmore fed my intense desire to make a difference. Swarthmore gave me the courage to follow my curiosity, even if I did not have a concrete plan for my career path. Swarthmore pushed me to embrace challenges rather than to play it safe. And, perhaps most important, Swarthmore friends helped me discern the moral threat Enron posed for me and helped me on my journey back to service to others.

෪෪

Cathy Abbott has left the corporate world to study at Wesley Theological Seminary with the intention of becoming a minister in the United Methodist Church.

The Stone in the Courtyard

T. Alexander Aleinikoff '74

I know a person who tries to make sure that when she climbs stairs, she always takes the last step with her right foot. She has no explanation for this; it's just the way she likes to climb stairs. Each of us has a ritual or two like this one—a certain way we put on our shoes or drink a cup of coffee.

My ritual at Swarthmore I will disclose here for the first time. The courtyard in front of Wharton is made up of large flagstones. There was one stone, just a few steps outside my entryway, that rocked a bit if you stepped diagonally from one corner to another. As I returned to my dorm room each night, I made sure that I stepped on that stone. I am not sure exactly what it was about that gently rocking stone, but to tread, rock, and then move on gave me the feeling of a certain, secure knowledge. Perhaps it made me feel that the Wharton quad was *my* home, holding a secret that I shared with it.

Taken as a metaphor, the ritual of the stone leads in many directions. It portrays the security Swarthmore provided (even as it challenged us); it reflects the sense that Swarthmoreans have of belonging to a secret society; it can stand for the idea that one "comes home" when one possesses certain knowledge. I believe all of these things, but it is the physical theme that I want to pursue. The stoneness. I have always thought that the Swarthmore alma mater began with an unduly dour phrase: "Staunch and gray thou standst before us." But I must concede that the words capture something deep about the College. The institution can appear forbidding, stern, judgmental.

Other words carved on a stone in the wall of Parrish Hall (located on the side closest to McCabe Library) convey a similar impression: "Use well thy freedom." But is not freedom exactly for *not* using well—for experimenting, for trying and failing, for getting outside oneself, for perceiving beyond knowledge? "Use well they freedom" raps our knuckles, calls us to our senses.

And yet, and yet . . . It is that message from Swarthmore that most remains with me. Read in a different light, it reminds us that the shortness of life is not inconsistent with the fullness of life. In fact, it doesn't really even caution against reckless abandon, if that's what the moment calls for. What it does demand of us is that we continue to ask ourselves the kind of difficult questions of which a Swarthmore education consists and for which a Swarthmore education has prepared us. Self-reflection—without self-absorption—is, to my mind, at the core of Swarthmore.

But Swarthmore is also more than this. It demands a looking in so that we may better go out. The College's Peace Collection signified this double sense for me. I liked to sit in the quiet of the collection and wander through its books and pamphlets that spoke so movingly of individual and collective action for peace. In some alchemical way, the calm contemplation forged iron-like commitments to seek to make the world more just.

I have tried to pursue the values that Swarthmore values—hard work, public service, intellectual curiosity, integrity—in my work as a law professor and as a federal-govern-

*In some alchemical way, the calm contemplation forged
iron-like commitments to seek to make the world more just.*

ment official. In one very particular way, Swarthmore has
directly influenced my academic career. In a seminar on
American Intellectual History, taught by Professor Robert
Bannister, we read an essay by Randolph Bourne titled
"Trans-national America." Bourne was a brilliant, radical social
critic who decried the support that the intelligentsia lent to
American war fever during World War I. Bourne also fought
against those who viewed immigration as a threat to
"American" values. Bourne argued that America's future
would be multicultural, with each new immigrant group contributing vibrant new threads to a national fabric forever in
the process of being woven. Bourne's essay speaks to modern
readers with the same freshness and urgency with which it
confronted readers several generations ago. And so, I found
myself rereading Bourne as I worked on a book that examines
constitutional-law issues relating to Indian tribes, the treat-
ment of immigrants, and the status of U.S. territories. My
book, *Semblances of Sovereignty* (published in 2002), ends by
quoting the Bourne essay that I first read more than 30 years
ago at Swarthmore.

Swarthmore is not all cold and gray stone. The newer
buildings display rosier tones, giving way to the playfulness of
the exterior of Kohlberg Hall. And there is real beauty in the
campus's gardens and trees, its long lawns and shaded walks. I
would like to think that as a student I appreciated the careful
placement and constant trimming of flora, but if I did so, it
was only in a subliminal way.

The implicit impact of the natural beauty of Swarthmore
is recalled by another stone that I remember from my days at

Swarthmore. Located above the amphitheater, it is engraved with a line from a Wordsworth poem: "Nature never did betray the heart that loved her." Here is a whole different side of Swarthmore.

I have always liked the poem that these words come from, "Lines Composed a Few Miles Above Tintern Abbey." In it, Wordsworth recalls scenes from his youth when he "bounded o'er the mountains, by the sides / Of the deep rivers." He writes, however, from the perspective of age—aware that his memories of nature have sustained him through more difficult times and that his life is closer to its end than its beginning. In his more mature mind's eye, the "groves and copses" take on a more subtle and sublime form. Nature is now "the anchor of my purest thoughts" and the "soul / Of all my moral being."

In a similar way, staunch and gray Swarthmore today yields up softer memories. The long reading assignments; the difficult paper topics; the anguished, existential late-night discussions are now recalled as the joys of learning and the source of the abiding importance of close friendships. These remembrances have surely helped sustain me in difficult days of adulthood, and they continue to attach me to the College. Though the wobble of the stones in Wharton's courtyard has now been repaired, for me one stone still gently rocks.

෯෯

Alex Aleinikoff, an expert on constitutional law and immigration law, is on the faculty of Georgetown University Law School.

Opening
the Door

Sherry Bellamy '74

As I write this essay, the U.S.
Supreme Court has just issued its landmark decision in *Grutter
v. Bollinger*, affirming the permissible use of race as a factor
when making decisions in admission to educational institutions. For the past few days, I have been engaged in an ongoing friendly debate with my boss and mentor about the meaning of affirmative action and its continuing validity. He objected to my statement that I was a beneficiary of affirmative
action—stating unequivocally that my degrees from
Swarthmore and Yale Law School made me as well qualified
as my peers in our corporation's legal department. I struggled
to explain to him that Justice Clarence Thomas' bizarre concern about the purported "stigma" of affirmative action was a
reflection of the justice's flawed psyche, and not a reason to
abandon a program that works. I feel neither stigma nor concern about benefiting from the only privilege that American
society has ever bestowed upon the descendants of African
slaves. I recognize that without the affirmative action practiced
by Swarthmore College in 1969, I would never have been in
a position to achieve what I have been fortunate enough to
have achieved.

Swarthmore sought me out. It aggressively looked for students of color and ability who could succeed and thrive in a rigorous academic atmosphere. To the College's great credit, however, it undertook its affirmative action in the same manner as it approaches all major efforts—with care and vigor in equal measure. Swarthmore sought to admit black students in numbers large enough to create a critical mass—not just to give us an opportunity to attend the institution but to ensure that we became a part of the institution. In contrast to so many colleges at which African American students felt alienated and discouraged, I felt at home at Swarthmore from the very first moment I stepped off the train and walked up Magill Walk. I know that my experience was not universal, but neither was it unique among my black classmates and those who followed us.

I did not come from the privileged backgrounds of so many of my classmates. My parents were low-level civil servants, and I was one of seven children reared in a small apartment in Harlem. I had attended an elementary school that I later learned was the poorest funded in the entire New York Archdiocese. I then attended a blue-collar Catholic high school in the Bronx, from which I was the first student to have the audacity to think that I could apply to Swarthmore, much less gain admission. When I told my guidance counselor that my first choice was Swarthmore, she laughed out loud. She advised me that I could "possibly" get into City College and if I truly wanted to go away to school, she would recommend Lincoln University because it was also in Pennsylvania. She made clear to me that—as the anti-affirmative action activists would say—I was not "traditionally" qualified to attend Swarthmore, and I should adjust my sights to something more attainable.

My reaction to that conference was to ignore her and to present to Swarthmore an application that I thought was unassailable. I knew that my high school education was challeng-

I feel neither stigma nor concern about benefiting from the only privilege that American society has ever bestowed upon the descendants of African slaves.

ing enough and my test scores were high enough, and thus my ambition recognized no boundaries. My application essay discussed the need to revise American-history curricula so that "black history" would not be relegated to the shortest, dreariest month of the year but would be integrated into the whole. I argued that one could not tell the story of America without including the story of the Africans who helped to shape it. In the spring of 1970, I received a letter advising that I had been admitted—early. I delivered that letter to my guidance counselor with no comment but with a very satisfied smirk.

So, when asked to write about the meaning of Swarthmore, I can only say that Swarthmore opened the doors to the rest of my life in ways in which the admissions officer who took a chance on my application could never have envisioned. Without any real understanding of what I was being given, I gained access to an education once reserved for only the privileged few—many of whom, although not all, were already in the upper class of American society. Before the late 1960s, very, very few Swarthmore students were persons of color.

I like to think that I took advantage of the opportunity. Certainly, I devoured information and ideas that had never been discussed in the rigid confines of my elementary and secondary education. I embraced the other activists within S.A.S.S. (the Swarthmore Afro-American Students Society), and I learned as much from my peers as from my professors. In some ways, I was not as engaged with the wider Swarthmore community as I should have been because I was still intimidated by many aspects of that environment.

Although I took what Swarthmore offered in smaller bites than I now wish I had, I was well fed nonetheless.

My memories of Swarthmore are almost all positive. Even the challenges had positive outcomes, and the painful experiences were infrequent but invaluable. Some of the memories are universal to my era at the school: the leather chairs at McCabe Library that were the ideal places to curl up and read assigned texts; the spring days on "Parrish Beach," watching Frisbee games; the Clothier Tower chimes, which were the gentlest reminder to hasten to your next class that one could imagine; the joy of reaching into the little brass mailboxes to find letters from home or from friends.

Some of my memories are uniquely from "Black at Swarthmore" and are equally cherished: time spent in the Black Cultural Center library, which was our own special trove of books that really mattered; performing with the Black Dance Ensemble and listening to the Gospel Choir, the two means of artistic expression started by our classes; sitting at the "black tables" at Sharples, which were our odd segregationist stance in the middle of an integrated community; tutoring my little sister, "Peaches," from the Ville, who was part of the black students' Big Sister Program; thriving on the endless friction caused by debates at S.A.S.S. meetings (the details of which I can never recall); and planning the "Ladies Tea" some of us hosted for the Swarthmore housemaids, which was one of the very first integrated events at the Black Cultural Center because not all of the cleaning ladies were black.

That tea caused its own source of friction among two of my more affluent—and thus more "cultured"—black classmates: They debated about the propriety of open finger sandwiches at the hour of 4 o'clock. The result was the closing of the sandwiches, followed by the angry reopening of the sandwiches—followed by my laughing so hysterically that I had to leave the kitchen. In the meantime, our guests, the maids who usually spent their time cleaning up after us, were waiting to be served. I don't remember now whether their sandwiches were served with or without tops, but I do remember that the guests were pleased to be treated as the ladies they were.

I owe much to Swarthmore that I can never repay. It taught me about myself and about the world community in which we all live. It taught me to appreciate the joy of learning and provided me with the tools to succeed. It taught me how to be a leader among my peers and how to advocate for our interests.

I must admit, however, that I still have no idea of the appropriate time of day after which one's sandwiches must be closed.

Sherry Bellamy, a vice president and associate general counsel of Verizon, is responsible for state regulatory matters.

I Have Learned
a Number
of Things

Joann Bodurtha '74

*J*une *2003, Virginia.* I am 50 years old. I have learned a number of things. Among them: Every human being deserves a good upbringing and respect. Teaching and expertise matter. I am grateful to be a doctor. I will die trying. How has Swarthmore influenced the unfolding of my genes? I find that my attempt to answer this question takes me on a journey through my memory that doesn't always run in chronological sequence.

September 1970, Swarthmore. The Career Office gives an aptitude test to incoming freshmen. Mine results in a tie score—I will be either a public speaker or a librarian. Is it off to McCabe for me, to talk in the library? My classmates are so capable, and my public high school preparation seems uneven. My German professor, Hilde Cohn, comments on my first essay: "Considering your limited ability, this little paper isn't bad." She smiles, and I believe that she is right. My math and physics professors, David Rosen and Mark Heald, are a bit more optimistic and dutifully sit through my questions during office hours. J. Roland Pennock and other faculty members have written the books we use in class. The possibilities of what we can do seem unlimited.

It is minus-17 degrees. The natives do not care that I went to Swarthmore.

September 1974, New Haven. During orientation, a professor suggests that MCATS and GPAs should be ignored, and new criteria for medical school admission should be used: Applicants should have lived in a foreign culture, been sick, and been in love. I will study at the Nagasaki University School of Medicine after my second year because Swarthmore administrators cared enough to remember me and nominate me for a Luce Scholarship. I've been reasonably healthy, but I did have firsthand experience with the effects of sickness when I was a fourth-grader—my father had a long bout with cancer and was out of work. Love? It remains a question mark. On the first day of medical school, I am sitting in the back of a cell-biology class. I cannot understand a word the professor is saying. Everyone in front of me is taking notes. I realize that everyone else somehow knew that medical school was conducted in Latin. Then I recognize the word "ribosome," and I realize this isn't Latin; the professor has been speaking with a thick Romanian accent. I know about ribosomes. Bob Savage and John Jenkins talked about them in biology and genetics classes at Swarthmore. I have a framework for organizing all this new material.

September 1971, Swarthmore. I am in a room of my own on the fourth floor of Parrish. My closest friends are leaving, one to be with her dying mother and the other to try to find out who she is besides a dutiful student. I have taken just one shot in my entire career on the junior varsity basketball team against Cheyney State—and made it. Two weeks as the leading scorer percentage-wise! I am the one white woman in a swimming class of city-bred or international students who

haven't had access to a pool. I am a lousy swimmer but initially the best among them. I am helping others not be afraid
of putting their face underwater. Math class is down to me,
two guys, and a Wang computer in DuPont. It is lonely, and I
am not as good and creative at math as I think I need to be. A
medical career, perhaps teaching genetics, might combine my
love of math; my public-speaking aptitude; and my need, driv-
en by childhood experiences, for a steady job.

June 1975, Philadelphia. Geneticists at the Children's
Hospital of Philadelphia (CHOP) have supported my application for a March of Dimes summer fellowship. I am at the
incubator of a premature child with Down syndrome, as the
scout for the geneticist. The head of pediatrics walks by with
a group of medical students. He asks who I am. I explain, and
then he asks me to tell the students about Down syndrome. It
is my third day at CHOP. I have stayed up late reading about
Down syndrome, but I am only a first-year medical student. I
almost demur, but then I remember the times at Swarthmore
when I didn't do well on exams but got back up again. I
remember going to Bryn Mawr on the tricollege bus to hear
Kate Millett talk about self-doubt and discovery. I remember
the admissions interviewer at Swarthmore asking me why I
had written my essay about my admiration for people who
made decisions but weren't self-righteous about them. I
explain Down syndrome to the Penn medical students.

September 1972, Swarthmore. I am dog-and-house sitting
for George and Maralyn Orbison Gillespie '49, who remain
models for us by gardening together and cultivating a life of
grace, humor, and spiced peaches. Maralyn has also hired me
to work in the Publications Office. I have a partial scholarship
but need to make money for books, so I also work in the dining hall and at the College's telephone switchboard. In the
summer, I had served ice cream at a Friendly's restaurant.
"Friendly? You bet we are. My name is Jo-jo." I had felt sorry
for myself, a Swarthmore student in a gray Puritan costume. I

told the manager that I wished I were Paul, the dishwasher, who could never quite learn to scoop ice cream. He told me never to say that. "To Paul, his problems are as big as Joann's are to her." George Fox and the Quakers talked about seeing the light in everyone.

Fall 1979, Philadelphia. I am a pediatric intern, tired and scurrying. A phone call interrupts rounds. My Swarthmore classmate Dan Brenner has died. When he had been hospitalized at Penn for seizures, we had disgusting yogurt-eating contests like the ones we had had in college. What kind of doctor can't even help her friends? Dan was bright, so caring, and different.

May 1982, Swarthmore, Friends Meetinghouse. I have discovered love. Tom and I get married, with Terry Shane and the Pennocks as our overseers. Tom had commuted to a state university in Ohio, had objected to the Vietnam War, and had taken principled stands on other things.

September 1985, Swarthmore. I am on the Board of Managers. In my career, I am beginning to understand the persuasive powers of money—I have entered the mature world, where a big part of my job is generating the resources for others to do their jobs and good work. At the College, I see the way others engage in the struggle to avoid cynicism and hypocrisy, and to keep Swarthmore admissions need blind, diverse, and responsive to the greater world.

January 1983, Turtle Mountain Reservation, N.D. It is minus 17 degrees—before windchill. The natives do not care that I went to Swarthmore or Yale. The children are beautiful, but many mothers are battered. I start a tiny breast-feeding support group, try to get better medicines for the pharmacy, and introduce an office-appointment system.

April 2003, Richmond, Va. I tell a family that their seizing newborn has a "smooth brain" and will likely remain babylike in development. I am grateful daily for the well-being of our 14-year-old daughter, Anna. The core of my job as a professor at an urban public university is handling interruptions—from student questions about genetics to patient crises and grant deadlines. Swarthmore gave me confidence that I could handle whatever would come before me, and the knowledge that teaching and expertise matter. It gave me a grounding in lifelong learning, addressing reality, and empathizing with the cast of characters that are at the core of being a doctor. My patients crowd my head as I try to figure out how to help them. We all are the products of a complex web of genes and environment. I wish all young adults could share in the nurturing provided by Swarthmore. My sense is that the gift of a Swarthmore education commits us to sharing what we can of the talents the College fostered in us.

⁂

Joann Bodurtha, a pediatrician and geneticist, teaches and does research at Virginia Commonwealth University.

A Way to Be of Use

Inés Lucía Cifuentes '75

It wasn't until I arrived at Swarthmore that I began to feel at home in this country. Some details about my childhood and family may help explain why.

I am the daughter of an Ecuadorian father and a North American mother from the Bronx. I grew up acutely aware of the powerful effects of race, ethnicity, and class, and the consequent inequities and injustices. My father was one of the early economists in Ecuador. My mother, Lucy Axelbank '45, attended Swarthmore on a scholarship at a time when there weren't many other Jews at the College. She majored in economics and later went to work at the Economic Commission for Latin America in Santiago, Chile. My parents met in Quito, where she was part of a mission to conduct the first economic study of Ecuador, and my father (who worked at the Central Bank) had been assigned to assist. Seven months later, they married and went to England, where my father studied at the London School of Economics—and where I was born. Before I began to speak or walk, I moved with my parents to Quito.

In Quito, I was the princess of the Cifuentes household, being the first grandchild. In less than two years, however, I was dethroned by the birth of my brother, Luis Cifuentes '78. From Ecuador we moved to Asunción, Paraguay, where I learned Guaraní and attended kindergarten. After two years there, we moved to Santiago, where I learned to read and write in both Spanish and English. A month after our arrival, the great Chilean earthquake of 1960 occurred. We felt it in Santiago and a year later visited Concepción, where I could see its effects—the coast had been lifted by about a meter. The earthquake was an event that had a profound impact on my educational and professional life. My study of it eventually, in 1988, became the topic of my Ph.D. thesis at Columbia University.

From Chile we moved to Guatemala, where my father worked with a former classmate from the London School of Economics, Alberto Fuentes Mohr, on a development program for Central America. There, I came into my own. I shed my cloak of shyness, had lots of friends, and was one of the best students. We left Guatemala City at the end of 1965 for Washington, D.C., just as the guerrillas were moving in and the violence that engulfed the country over the next decades was becoming established. Fourteen years later, Alberto Fuentes Mohr was assassinated by paramilitary forces.

I attended public schools in Montgomery County, Md. There weren't many students who looked like me at Kensington Junior High School—at that time, the school district was about 70 percent white. One day, in gym class, the teacher ordered me to take off my nylons. I had to tell her that I wasn't wearing any—it was the color of my skin. She didn't apologize, and I was devastated. I retreated into my studies and into books that were written in Spanish or French. I yearned for Latin America and planned to return to live and work there.

Then, in 1971, I arrived at Swarthmore. I reveled in the exchange of ideas in my classes, over meals, and late at night in our rooms. I remember sitting over dinners in Sharples with

David Sacks '76 while we told each other Greek myths; listening to Danny Allen '79, as he stared at his hands, telling me about his grandmother and how he didn't feel at home in this country, where he and his ancestors had been born; hearing jazz for the first time; watching Denise Dennis '72 act the balcony scene from *Romeo and Juliet* in McCabe.

I loved being in a place where ideas mattered. Ken Mills, a visiting professor who taught Marxist philosophy, challenged our ideas, forced us to grapple with the way we lived our lives, and questioned the nature of our relationships—between professors and students, between men and women, between those of us who studied at the College and those who worked there. I recall an attempt to unionize the women who cleaned our rooms and the men who cleaned the rest of the College buildings—most of whom were African American—and being struck by what one of the men said at a meeting. He told us simply that he wanted to be treated with respect, to be acknowledged as a person.

At the age of 7 or 8, when I was living in Chile, I had decided that I wanted to become an astronomer, and so I majored in physics at Swarthmore and took astrophysics courses at Haverford. I was intrigued by black holes, the nature of the universe, and cosmology, but I found that I do not have the kind of mathematical mind that is needed to uncover more about the universe. Earthquakes still fascinated me, and Professor Paul Mangelsdorf '49 suggested that I consider doing graduate work in earth science. He recommended that I apply to schools where I could study both earth science and astrophysics. I entered the Geophysics Department at Stanford University in 1976 after a summer spent in Mexico City researching the Mexicanization Law with Professor Ken Sharpe of Swarthmore. This experience convinced me that political science could be just as esoteric as astrophysics and reinforced my determination to continue in science while seeking a way to be of use to people in Latin America.

I loved being in a place where ideas mattered.

While I was struggling with the questions about what I wanted to do and become, I wrote to several of my parents' friends in Latin America and asked them for advice. Alberto Fuentes Mohr showed the letter to an Argentinean friend and physicist. He said: "Tell her it doesn't matter what she does as long as she does it well. She will find a way to be of use." He was right.

I now direct the Carnegie Academy for Science Education (CASE). In 1989, when Maxine Frank Singer '52 became president of the Carnegie Institution of Washington, she opened a Saturday science school for elementary-age children from two neighborhood public schools. The children at the First Light School, as it was called, began to do better in their schools, and some of the Latino students began to speak in English. One of the principals and some parents asked Maxine whether Carnegie could teach their schools' teachers to teach in this way, and the National Science Foundation (NSF) invited Maxine to submit a proposal. It was December 1992, and I had run out of funds to continue my research on large earthquakes. Vera Rubin, a Carnegie astronomer and a wonderful mentor of many young scientists, suggested that Maxine get in touch with me. I wrote the proposal to NSF, and we established CASE in December 1993.

For 10 years, we have provided the only sustained high-quality professional development in science and mathematics available to public school elementary teachers in the District of Columbia. We have nurtured a group of mentor teachers who excel in our program, love to teach science and mathematics, and are committed to their students. They are proof to other teachers that students in D.C. public schools can excel academically when their teachers have high expectations of them and are committed to their academic success. They and the children are the reason I have stayed in this job, even though it is not what I ever imagined I would be doing at this stage of my life and is the most difficult work I have ever done.

Over the years, Swarthmore students have interned at CASE during the summer. Jennifer Lee '98, Victor Pineiro '00, Karman Mak '00, and Naamal De Silva '00—from four different cultural backgrounds—all carry inside them the desire to use their talents and education to make the world a better place. I don't know exactly how it happens—whether it is the students who apply to Swarthmore; the College's selection process; or the ethos of high intellectual demands, with responsibility to others, nurtured by professors for whom the teaching of young people is a passion. All I know is that these factors have conjoined to bring forth many of us who cannot accept things as they are and are working to change them for the better.

⁂

Inés Cifuentes, a seismologist, is the director of the Carnegie Institution's Carnegie Academy for Science Education.

Searching
for Beauty

Harold "Koof" Kalkstein '78

If they knew of her impact, those I work with would be upset with Connie Hungerford. But they would be nearly 30 years too late. The seed she planted so long ago is what now compels my move from a hectic work pace to a slower life—an aesthetic life. Instead of solving business problems, I will be searching out beauty in all its forms, while trying to figure out how I can create some on my own in the process. How did it happen that today, at the age of 47, I am affected by Swarthmore as profoundly as I was when I was a student?

My introduction to the College came in the form of cold, crisp afternoons watching football. Two older brothers played on the team, and they, as well as my parents and sister, preceded me to Swarthmore. It seemed to be a fine place for them. For me, it seemed to be a logical school to visit, to get a practice interview in preparation for whatever college I would really want to attend. But as I went through the application process and got to know Swarthmore for myself, I found that it was the college I really wanted to go to.

I majored in economics and minored in political science. The honors seminars were the defining aspect of the College for me. Being up close and personal with six to eight students and a professor, and having to write a paper or two a week (with no word processor to fix one's grammar and spelling mistakes), was an excellent training ground for thinking and communicating. The ability to think on one's feet—to always have a logic, a story, for what you were focused on—was a skill Swarthmore instilled in me. And being able to argue vociferously with friends and then let it all go is a wonderful way to learn that friendship and community are not based on shared views but, rather, on shared values.

Fulfilling distribution requirements led me to an introductory art history course, taught by a new assistant professor who—nervously, at first—walked us through the basics of the development of painting, sculpture, and architecture. She knew her stuff well but seemed to come alive when we reached impressionism. My term paper, based on a Monet painting I had seen only in a photographic reproduction, was not well thought out. In discussing the paper with me, Professor Hungerford gently but firmly made the point that I would get a lot more out of art if I would find a way to go and see it, and take it in fully, using both my mind and my feelings. At the time, her comments washed over me—after all, I had passed the course.

Swarthmore was fun and a great learning experience. I benefited from the subjects taught, the friendships formed and maintained, and the experience of learning to live independent of my family. Swarthmore allowed me to express my curiosity and my desire to explore. By graduation, however, the notion of an aesthetic life was very far removed from my consciousness; I was ready to go to work.

For the past 20 years, that work has taken the form of management consulting. It has covered many types of problems, including the acquisition or divestiture of businesses, the building of new businesses, the streamlining of existing operations, and the redesign of organizations. Getting the logic

What will my son learn? What seed will be planted in him?

right and telling the story are the key skills of a consultant, and I have become quite good at them, thanks to the jump start those honors papers and seminars gave me.

In my profession, the real key to success is the ability to develop such skills in others. Holding others to high intellectual standards, helping more junior consultants think about the logic and the story, and teaching them to have empathy for others are all critical. In fostering this development, I found that I relied heavily on the techniques that several of my professors, such as Frank Pierson, had used.

I have worked across many industries and have undertaken numerous pro bono assignments, ranging from efforts to revitalize the city of Oakland to helping nonprofit organizations that advocate for the improvement of children's welfare and education. As the old Quaker saying goes, I have done good and, in the process, done well. But it has been a grueling life, involving much travel and inflicting hardships on my wife (whom I met in Washington and married while attending business school) and two children (the older of whom now attends Swarthmore).

Two summers ago, I had the opportunity to take a sabbatical for 10 weeks. My family and I toured parts of Eastern Europe, Germany, Italy, France, and Scotland. In the course of the trip, I came to realize that many of the sights were familiar from my art history course. Without having planned it, I was, at last, following Professor Hungerford's advice on slowly letting the works of art and architecture permeate my brain and my soul.

I toured Ireland alone during the last week of my sabbatical. In Ireland, the art and architecture are less magisterial than those I had encountered in other places, but there is great natural beauty. And there are wonderful ruins, not grand or immense, but accessible and alive. Wandering through them, and around the countryside, I came to a full realization of my desire to experience more beauty and to take on the challenge of attempting to create a bit of it myself.

Since the sabbatical, I have been fulfilling the remaining responsibilities I have to my partners and am now ready to embark on the next phase of my life. What will this life contain? I can't say for sure, but I do know there are many beautiful areas to explore still. And while I can't paint, I think I can build things that create beauty, such as a Victorian garden. Mostly, I hope to conduct my life at a pace that allows me to feel all of its rich possibilities.

As for Swarthmore, I know it will continue to affect me. I am now on the Alumni Council, and my son has three more years to go; so there will be many connections in the coming years. I do wonder about what lies ahead. What will I still learn? What will my son learn? What seed will be planted in him?

🕮

Koof Kalkstein is a senior partner with the Boston Consulting Group in San Francisco.

A Sense
of Self

Wilma Lewis '78

Swarthmore was my first real adventure living in a world that was different from the one to which I was accustomed: the small island of St. Thomas, U.S. Virgin Islands, where I grew up. Despite a solid foundation—close family ties, a loving and supportive upbringing, graduation from a highly regarded private school with high honors and as valedictorian of my senior class, numerous athletics awards, and active church and community involvement—I found myself facing this new adventure with some trepidation. I couldn't help wondering just where, and how, this 18-year-old kid from the Caribbean would fit in. I couldn't help questioning whether I would be able to compete academically and in other ways at an institution like Swarthmore College.

As I reflect on my four years at Swarthmore, I realize that there are several principles that guide my life today that can be traced, at least in part, to the sense of self that I developed as I navigated this new world. Some of these principles include the words of St. Francis De Sales, who said, "Do not wish to be anything but what you are, and try to be that perfectly"; the thoughts of Mary McLeod Bethune, who emphasized the importance of having a "strong belief in ourselves and our possibilities"; and the insights of Ralph Waldo Emerson, who reminded us that "What lies behind us and what lies before us are tiny matters compared to what lies within us." By successfully navigating the Swarthmore environment—graduating with distinction and Phi Beta Kappa, receiving the Joshua Lippincott Fellowship, lettering in three varsity sports, participating in other extracurricular activities, and making lifelong friends—I was well on my way to cultivating that sense of self that would enable me to embrace these principles and shape my world.

There are many experiences that I had at Swarthmore that were likely contributors to this outcome. Perhaps it started at the very beginning, when my parents and I met Swarthmore alumna Barbara Pearson Lange [Godfrey] '31 at a freshman orientation gathering. Mrs. Lange was the daughter of Paul Pearson, the first civilian governor of the Virgin Islands and a former professor at Swarthmore to whom my father had often referred in encouraging me to attend the College. Maybe our chance encounter with Mrs. Lange, with her ties to the Virgin Islands, gave me my first sense of "belonging."

Possibly, it was the selfless dedication of members of the faculty, such as Professor David Rosen, who conducted voluntary study sessions every Tuesday and Thursday, when our freshman math class was not in session. As was typical of the Swarthmore faculty, Professor Rosen gave that something extra to encourage us to develop our abilities to the fullest.

Perhaps it was the personal interest in my development shown by members of the administration. Assistant Dean Janet Dickerson, for example, always found time to invite my roommate and me into her office just to chat—sometimes for hours—when she saw us wandering the halls of Parrish during our freshman year.

Maybe the courage to reach to the outer limits of my capabilities was fostered by the extremely high academic stan-

*I couldn't help wondering just where, and how,
this kid from the Caribbean would fit in.*

dards to which we were held by our incredibly talented faculty and the gentle prodding to go even beyond from such people as Associate Provost Gil Stott, whose words of encouragement led to my application for a Rhodes Scholarship.

Perhaps it was the stimulating discussions—both in and out of the classroom—among the intellectually gifted students, which taught me to appreciate the diversity of opinions while also valuing my own individual contribution.

Possibly, my sense of self was fueled by the opportunity to celebrate and share the African American heritage at a predominantly white institution through membership in the Swarthmore College Gospel Choir, which performed to standing-room-only crowds at the Friends Meetinghouse and whose members were always made to feel very special—both individually and collectively—by the undying support of our most loyal fan, Ann Geer, a College employee.

Maybe I was influenced by the spirit of healthy competition derived from playing varsity basketball, tennis, and volleyball at an institution that allowed us to develop and showcase our athletic skills but also to learn that there is more to the game than the final score and more to the season than the won-lost record.

Whatever the combination of factors, the rich Swarthmore experience has fueled a continuing desire to develop my own talents and abilities, a passion for reaching deep within to give my very best, and the courage to face new challenges with a strong belief in myself and my possibilities. I relied on this sense of self in pursuing my legal education at Harvard; in rising to the challenge of serving for almost three years as inspector general of the U.S. Department of the Interior, managing and supervising a headquarters office and 11 field offices; in assuming the daunting role of U.S. attorney for the District of Columbia for more than three years, leading the largest of the country's 93 U.S. attorney's offices, with more than 350 assistant U.S. attorneys, an equal number of support staff, and the unique responsibility of serving as both federal and local prosecutor; and now, in navigating the world of private practice as a partner at Crowell & Moring LLP in Washington, D.C.

When I think about Swarthmore, I have lots to be thankful for because the College has contributed immeasurably to the person I am today.

⁂

Wilma Lewis, who served as U.S. attorney for the District of Columbia, is now in private practice in Washington, D.C.

Talking for a Living

America Rodriguez '78

I talk for a living. For 10 years after graduation, I worked as a broadcast journalist, first as a reporter for the National Public Radio (NPR) affiliate in Philadelphia, WHYY-FM, and then as a Los Angeles–based correspondent for the network. I loved my NPR job, but I wanted to change the rhythms of my life. I began to think about going back to school.

Exploring my options, I set up an "informational interview" with the chair of the Department of Communication at the University of California–San Diego. In his office, hanging on the wall from a garnet-colored cord, was a familiar calendar. Beaming, I introduced myself, adding "Class of '78." Michael Schudson smiled back and replied, "Class of '69." Of course, this was just a coincidence. On that day 20 years ago, I was uncertain, wondering whether leaving journalism and becoming a professor was the right choice for me. The Swarthmore link between Michael and me clinched the decision. I was home. Michael went on to chair my dissertation committee, and today he is one of my most valued friends and colleagues.

The commonality of the Swarthmore experience—the

resiliency of that bond—is not merely a sentimental one. It is also about the assumptions we make about each other. (The social scientist in me is whispering, "Careful now. . . .") We Swarthmoreans love reading, writing, asking questions, sharing the answers, and then asking more questions. That can be said about most people who have had good liberal arts educations. What makes Swarthmore distinctive—what the meaning of Swarthmore is for me—is the heightened awareness of broad social and historical forces, the self-consciousness that the College encourages in its students.

At Swarthmore's core is a paradox. From the meticulously tended Rose Garden to the [former] maid service in its dormitories, Swarthmore is more than comfortable; materially, it is elite. Yet at the same time, there is an awareness of the social injustices of our world—and of our responsibility to use our privileges to right these imbalances. Swarthmore's Quaker heritage, although never emphasized, was always—is always— a central theme of my Swarthmore experience.

I was a double major in English and Spanish literature. Sipping sherry in Professor Derek Traversi's living room while discussing Shakespeare's sonnets, and Rioja in Phil Metzidakis' dining room while discussing *Don Quixote*, are clear memories and inspirations for me today. If there was one class that represents my teaching ideals, it would be John Hassett's Latin American literature class, where we argued passionately about the role of the United States in the Allende coup in Chile. Given that I teach at the University of Texas at Austin (52,000 students), I feel fortunate when I am able to re-create a bit of Swarthmore in my home during a graduate seminar.

Back to talking for a living: In classes, seminars, and meals in Sharples, I learned to talk on my feet. This ability has been reinforced countless times over the years, but its germ was Swarthmore. It came in handy when, in the same day, I had to report on stories ranging from community activists in Watts to Edwin Meese, President Reagan's attorney general. That calm,

> *We, in all our multidimensional diversity,*
> *are the meaning of Swarthmore.*

deliberate confidence is also helpful now when I address 500 sleepy adolescents from behind a lectern.

When I was a full-time journalist, I traced my ability to write under pressure to the second semester of my sophomore year, when I wrote four research papers in less than a week. I have happy memories of that week—and not only because I lived to tell the tale. Several of us, most of whom were members of the steering committee of the Alice Paul Women's Center, moved into a large sitting room in the center with our sleeping bags, typewriters (which some of you remember), cans of tuna, and boxes of macaroni and cheese. Although I don't think we ever said so out loud, we felt that the spirit of Alice Paul (Class of 1905) was with us. In 1923, she was the author of the original Equal Rights Amendment.

Alice Paul's Swarthmore descendants—men and women—continue to build a bridge between a liberal arts philosophy and workaday routines in classrooms, offices, and politics. In other words, we, in all our multidimensional diversity, are the meaning of Swarthmore.

America Rodriguez teaches in the Departments of Radio-TV-Film and Journalism at the University of Texas.

Screaming for No Apparent Reason

John Brady Kiesling '79

Was I screaming "Nuke them!" or only "Bomb them!" as I sprinted into the control room in Trotter during the waning seconds of the poli-sci international-relations simulation? My memory is untrustworthy. But I remember clearly that my machinations as defense minister and U.N. representative of the African Front Line states bore bitter fruit in this, my first and last international-relations course. I had blithely lied to my South African counterpart, luring him into his cross-border provocation that legitimized a Soviet invasion to free the oppressed African peoples. My glacial Soviet protector, however, had just lost five armored divisions in an uncharted swamp west of Cape Town as play was ending.

Ah, Secretary Rumsfeld, I was young and stupid, awash in hormones and with a distribution requirement to fulfill, but what was *your* excuse? No, seriously, it was an excellent class, like most Swarthmore classes. But was I better suited then—a classics major caught up in an adolescent game—to represent a new American Empire than I found myself to be 20-odd years later as a professional diplomat promoting our invasion of Iraq as the political counselor at the U.S. Embassy in

Athens? Sometimes I think so. I foundered on an administration that prides itself on its brutally "realistic" foreign policy. That realism has little to do with the definitions of realism I studied in philosophy class. It is a realism that maps the real world about as precisely as did the "Dungeons and Dragons" fantasy campaigns I lived through at Swarthmore. The results are no more morally uplifting than those of my poli-sci role-playing exercise, and the security our realism purports to offer is a mirage or worse.

Security is a legitimate hunger. Swarthmore College was and remains dutifully *in loco parentis*, attempting to persuade the student body that its landscaped little universe seethes with menace. In my day, this attempt was subverted, rather than reinforced, by the campus security reports prominently posted each week. Yes, there was a rape attempt, and we large males were deputized to walk women friends home in the dark. There was an off-campus suicide, pilferage from the dorms, and the ransacking of the campus dope dealer's room when his relations with the Warlocks went through a delicate phase. But those security reports lingered in my memory as an accidentally poetic embellishment of a benign landscape: Each new spring, freshmen would spot the "naked man in the Crum"; almost every week, the overweight police pensioners on their underpowered golf carts would dutifully pursue reports of "screaming for no apparent reason." This last phrase, read on the dorm bulletin boards many times over my four years, was to stick in my mind, a general-purpose metaphor for the human condition.

We insist, in tones that brook no rational discussion, that the world has changed since Sept. 11, 2001. Has the world, in fact, gotten more dangerous? More dangerous than the Swarthmore it was and it remains. Still, all my diplomatic experience, all my reading of the world's bloody history, made me confident that, until we began our slide into war with Iraq, we had succeeded in making America as safe as any state at any time. The planet was dominated politically, economically, and militarily by ourselves and our allies. Growing networks of international law were fortified by bonds of economic interdependency without precedent. Terrorism indeed posed a disproportionate threat to Americans compared with Western Europeans, but the absolute magnitude was small, and the disproportion could be reduced by wiser diplomacy and by using existing institutions more effectively. I resigned from the State Department at the end of February 2003, as it became absolutely clear that we were not interested in reducing the threat but rather had chosen to increase the threat as the price for legitimizing the outcome of an internal Washington policy struggle that could not be legitimized analytically or morally.

Legitimacy is a hunger. For most of us, happiness inheres in knowing what we are supposed to do and doing it, knowing who our leaders are and following them. I arrived at Swarthmore with a hazy faith that the universe had rules, that it would unveil those rules to a mind sufficiently precise, patient, and detached. I was lured early into the microcosm of Greek and Latin, seduced by that small principality in which classics professors Martin Ostwald and Gil Rose knew the set of knowable rules and seemed to derive their great good humor from that knowledge. But a budding academic career was haunted by the fear that the secret rules of the broader universe might not be learnable inside the academy.

One rule crept out from Patrick Henry's Early Christianity seminar. As our little circle dissected the first generations of Christianity, I was illuminated by a revelation a more sociable child would have grasped in kindergarten—that legitimacy, whether human or divine, emanates from the dynamics of the group. The early Christians, like my little group of "Dungeons and Dragons" players, generated legitimacy from the interplay of insiders and outsiders, of dominance and submission, of violence and altruism. Later, I learned that evolutionary psychology used the game theory of successful primate hunter-gatherers to generalize the logic of group dynamics. On the African savannas, and inside even the most democratic of governing institutions, successful violence is the first and most potent source of legitimacy. It is not the only one.

Swarthmore is a paradise for small, intense groups and for the sense of unity and purpose such groups generate. We students saw the warm and fuzzy side of that—romping on our green hilltop, we hunted, gathered, and mated in a world of seemingly unlimited resources and only the most genteel competition, whether intellectual or reproductive. Should I be ashamed to admit that my vision of America, carefully nurtured through years abroad as a diplomat, resembled Swarthmore far more than it did the real America of duct tape and permits for concealed handguns? It was a useful delusion. If I was lying to gullible foreigners, selling them the "city on the hill" of a previous president's now discarded vision, I did not know I was lying, and my buttoned-down passion and classical syntax made me dangerously plausible. When I returned from each overseas posting to brief stints as a State Department bureaucrat, it was to a pleasant liberal enclave of Northwest D.C. with a sufficiency of idealistic colleagues and with the potholes not too dire a reminder of the mean streets that, in foreign countries, I thought I had come to understand pretty well.

I had not been a pacifist when I came to Swarthmore, and I was not one when I graduated. I am not one now. Still, a more dangerous and conventional environment than Swarthmore's might have toughened me for official service in post–Sept. 11 America. I managed to advance in the Foreign Service without developing any zeal for the bureaucratic battles that are vital in placing the combatants within the small-group hierarchy of dominance and submission. I preferred to focus on what I thought was the proper sphere of diplomacy: the world outside the blast-proof walls of the U.S. Embassy. In

> *My vision of America resembled Swarthmore far more than it did the real America of duct tape and permits for concealed handguns.*

crueler surroundings than Swarthmore's, I would have been forced to prize, as threatened primates are deeply conditioned to prize, the instinct of group solidarity over that of intellectual integrity. The lies leaders tell to mobilize followers and allies serve, perhaps, a useful purpose, with a vital caveat: Those leaders should have a functional understanding of the environment in which they operate. But my own functional understanding of a less threatening world did not lend itself to such group dynamics. I could not be a player in this game.

Swarthmore admits no contradiction between idealism and realism, between truth and expediency. In an overpopulated world of finite resources, it is realistic to look at the case studies for success and failure and to admit that unpoliticized analysis, close cooperation, and more efficient organization are a price we must pay to keep so many expensive humans alive. The freedom from realism a little group of Beltway ideologues think it has achieved through the overwhelmingness of U.S. military power is the most dangerous fantasy imaginable. Swarthmoreans are not so different from other Americans in believing in humankind. We have no taste—or talent—for imperialism, and even our moralizing version is too expensive a game to continue playing as badly as we have.

The assigned essay topic is "The Meaning of Swarthmore." Writing now as a temporary expatriate in the shadow of the Acropolis, I would give Swarthmore as much and as little meaning as the ruined Parthenon that looms above me, entangled in its modern scaffolding. Each passing group imposes its own meaning in its own time and to its own purposes. Some basic common humanity assures, however, a certain common agreement that this is an enduring and powerful symbol, a beacon to be maintained at almost any cost.

Although I put Swarthmore aside for many years, it shone—and shines—in my memory as a generously tended vision on the hill, an enclave of American civility, a paradise of the changing seasons. The campus security guards were wise enough in 1979, or lazy enough, not to delve too deeply into why anyone would scream at Swarthmore. I witnessed enough on-campus screaming to attest that it seemed to make sense at the time, if only within the context of our little primate band. Humans are as yet imperfectly adapted to life in paradise. Like other primates, we scream occasionally when no mortal danger lurks. Unlike other primates, we are remorselessly rationalizing animals. Intellectual fashion and political expediency now urge that we import real or imaginary serpents into the paradise we labored to build. It may be more rational to settle for "screaming for no apparent reason" as all the explanation we can afford to demand.

Brady Kiesling, who resigned from the State Department to protest the war with Iraq and other policies, now writes and speaks on foreign-policy issues.

Introduction to Overanalysis

Rachel Weinberger '80

OK, I admit it: I was a mainstream Swarthmore student. Nothing out of the ordinary about me—no social causes, no unusual majors, no strong politics, no groundbreaking research. Just a girl from New Jersey who was pure liberal arts. With a major in art history—not even honors—I gobbled up as many art, music, history, and literature classes as I could, and decided to worry about a career later.

After graduation, I was torn between my love for the arts and the desire to make enough money to have a comfortable life. I clearly recall trying (unsuccessfully) to persuade a Morgan Stanley interviewer that my overdeveloped analytical skills were completely applicable to their intern program and that my lack of financial/economics classes—not abundantly available in our ivory tower—wouldn't be a deterrent.

In frustration, I went to business school in search of a degree that would get me a job. And it did. In 1983, having an M.B.A. was a significant qualification, and I got a job at a major New York bank—one that has since been eaten up by larger international institutions. But throughout my career, a Swarthmore education has been what mattered most. I consistently heard that although anyone could learn the technical skills, it was my ability to communicate effectively and to develop relationships that distinguished me.

While I was an average student academically, I did manage to sail through what I think of as "Introduction to Overanalysis" and "Advanced Overanalysis." My husband (a William and Mary graduate) is convinced that to get through four years at Swarthmore, we all had to excel in overanalysis and nurture a propensity to be extraordinarily verbal, if not verbose. To me, that's the essence of Swarthmore: our ability to communicate, whether by oral or written word, musical word, scientific word, philosophical word, English or ancient Greek word—it doesn't matter. It's what we do best, what is inherently part of us. And it's the purest definition of liberal arts.

As a high school senior, I was accepted by both Swarthmore and Bryn Mawr. I visited the two schools to figure out where I'd be happier. At Swarthmore, I had dinner with a group of freshmen with whom I then spent the evening, talking endlessly about whatever was critical to 17 and 18 year olds in 1976. I felt comfortable, as if I'd found a home, and I told my parents I was going to Swarthmore because I'd met people like me—exactly the kind of friends I wanted.

A few weeks into my freshman year, as I was talking late into the night with some sophomore women, I realized they were part of the group with whom I'd had dinner during that visit a few months earlier. Now, 27 years later, two of them remain my most cherished friends. We still have long conversations, obsessing over details and, of course, analyzing whatever it is we're discussing—children, careers, family, books, movies, food, music, the occasional foray in politics. Beyond them, there are other more distant Swarthmore friends with whom I'm always able to pick up our conversation as if we had spoken, written, or e-mailed just the day before.

The courses I remember best involved analysis and com-

> *I remember sometimes feeling like the Austrian archduke in* Amadeus *who tells Mozart that his opera has "too many notes."*

munication: Professor Metzidakis' Spanish literature class in my freshman year, where I struggled to be as fluently articulate in Spanish as in English; an intense historiography seminar with Professor Kitao in which we debated whether Michelangelo was an atheist; a paper I presented for double credit in Greek Art and Archeology with Connie Hungerford, in which I analyzed the painting and pigments on various Greek vases; Bernie Smith's Medieval History class, where we discussed the finer points of Benedictine and Cistercian monks; and Peter Swing's History of Music class, where the analysis of musical phrases was as difficult as what my friends were doing in Physical Chemistry. I remember sometimes feeling—especially during a long night writing art history papers—like the Austrian archduke in the play and movie *Amadeus,* who tells Mozart that his opera has "too many notes," or, in my case, words.

But my years at Swarthmore were about so much more than classes. When I left for college, my father paraphrased Mark Twain and told me not to let my classes get in the way of my education. And I didn't. Today, it makes me tired to think that when I was 18 years old, I sat in the amphitheater until 4 a.m., talking. The talking—at meals, in the library, between classes, and well into the night—is what I remember more than anything.

And here we are today. After 20 years in the financial-services industry, I've become a victim of the economy, forced to close the office I was running. For the first time since leaving graduate school, I don't have a job, and I lost this one at the height of my career. Much to my surprise, I realize that if

I don't return to this particular career, it doesn't matter. I'm still the same person because my family and friends, my upbringing, and my education shaped who I am. That overdeveloped ability to think clearly, speak articulately, write thoughtfully, read constantly, and, yes, analyze everything is with me—no matter what the external circumstances.

It seems to be time to return to my roots and find something more creative that will allow me to use fully the skills that were honed at Swarthmore. Perhaps what I do next will play to my liberal arts core—something that contributes more to society than designing a tax-efficient estate plan for someone with millions of dollars.

That's the other thing about many of us late-1970s to mid-1980s graduates: If we go in a direction that is not socially responsible, we are often pulled back. I always wanted to make a difference somehow, and now I am aware that I am doing so. I'm not going to expunge terrorism, bolster the economy, cure Parkinson's disease, or discover the lost island of Atlantis, but I have changed the lives of the people I love—and those who love me.

And in that pursuit, I am fueled by the things that are for me the essence of Swarthmore: the need and ability to communicate—and the lasting friendships I formed there.

🐟

Rachel Weinberger has held management positions
at several financial institutions.

Surrounded by Trees and Opinions

Iqbal Quadir '81

What did Swarthmore do for me? It freed my mind.

The lessons I learned at Swarthmore play a larger role in my life than the excellent courses I took there. The College taught me not to rely on standard education, not to drown myself in conventional wisdom, and not to lose sight of what really matters. It was a vital support for me and also an effective model that I was able to use later to solve problems of public service.

To explain that, let me first go back to my childhood and give proper credit to what I learned in rural Bangladesh, where I spent most of 1971—a momentous year in my life—and to my father, who paid a lot of attention to me during my formative years.

I grew up in a middle-class family. My father was a successful lawyer in Jessore, a town of approximately 100,000 in the 1960s. He was exceptionally knowledgeable about the world and its politics and economics. From the time I was about age 9, he enjoyed expounding his views on diverse subjects to me, his most admiring fan. These mind-expanding sessions were the happiest moments of my life.

Then, in 1971, the rhythm of our lives was harshly interrupted by civil war that brought extensive violence, especially in urban areas, and eventually created independent Bangladesh out of the eastern province of Pakistan. The fighting forced us to flee our town to settle in a remote village. Thanks to an absence of good roads and other means of communication, we were protected from the war, which tended to spread along highways, railroads, and rivers. At the same time, I realized that the absence of infrastructure held the people back from economic prosperity. I saw how the quality of life worsened as the war suspended the movement of goods and people. Then, when the war ended, I also saw how conditions improved as people were able to move and communicate again.

That year gave me a sense of life outside the urban pockets in Bangladesh, where only 10 percent of its population lived. In the midst of the sufferings of 1971, my father repeatedly pointed out that the general population, although poor, was the best source of ideas for enhancing its own well-being but was being kept poor by the powerful few, who were also causing the pain of that year.

However, 1971 was only the beginning of my problems. My father died in an accident in 1972. A devastating flood in 1974 put most of Bangladesh under water. Military coups in 1975 created even more uncertainties. As a result, I decided to venture abroad for education and chose America as my destination.

By 1976, when I was 18, I enrolled in a junior college in the American Midwest that waived my tuition fees. My mother found enough money for a plane ticket and a thousand dollars to cover my expenses for the first semester. I came to America without a long-term financial arrangement because I could not have made one. Luckily, my school performance led to increased financial aid and a confident search for a four-year college. In 1978, Swarthmore rescued me with full financial support.

At Swarthmore, I was surrounded by trees and opinions, increasing my respect for both. These trees, wearing their own name tags, had witnessed many debates in the shade of their boughs, and their discreet silence softened those exchanges of opinions. In the dining hall and in dormitories, where the debates were not moderated by trees—or teachers—the exchanges were more heated, and I was challenged from many directions. The result was my realization that the world was more complex than I had thought and that one's views benefit by being checked against those of others.

One such view was that the poverty in Bangladesh was caused merely by a lack of material things. This had led me to major in engineering and to choose Swarthmore because, unlike other liberal arts colleges, it had an Engineering Department. While I completed my degree in engineering, my discussions with students from diverse backgrounds led me to question my pursuit of technical competence. I started reading history and politics. Indeed, today at the John F. Kennedy School of Government at Harvard University, where I teach, I pay considerable attention to European medieval history to see how societies began to establish better ways of governing themselves, removing blockages to economic and social progress. In medieval Europe, technological progress allowed people to be more productive and led to the dispersion of power and to better governance. The empowerment of citizens from below led to property rights, capitalism, and democracy.

After Swarthmore, I earned a master's degree in economics from the Wharton School and worked for two years at the World Bank. But my independent study of history made me see a serious disconnect between World Bank-backed, state-led development efforts and the ways in which economies actually have developed. Foreign aid to developing countries that was used to fund state-led efforts empowered authorities, not citizens, centralizing power, as opposed to dispersing it.

The rhythm of our lives was harshly interrupted by civil war that brought extensive violence.

I came to the realization that the best way to advance poor countries is to pay attention to their poor citizens directly, by helping them to become more productive and, in turn, to assert their rights. By asserting their rights, they have a louder voice in determining how they should be governed. In contrast, external support that strengthens governments can potentially lead to actions contrary to the needs and wishes of citizens. As I thought about how to provide direct help to citizens, Swarthmore occupied my mind prominently. Its support, which enabled me to study there, was a clear example of private initiative for public good. Swarthmore laid the foundation for my faith in serving public ends through private initiatives, which can act as a countervailing force to public institutions—and a check against their possible abuse—while remaining weak enough to have to prove themselves continually.

Furthermore, appreciating how businesses have historically woven the economic fabric of today's developed countries, I returned to Wharton to pursue an M.B.A., and then worked in investment banking and venture capital in New York in the late 1980s. In the early 1990s, this financial experience, combined with my childhood exposure to rural Bangladesh, prompted me to recognize that the digital revolution could facilitate the introduction of telephones to 100 million people living in that area.

I set out to establish a business to provide these telephones. Many advised me to consider charity and subsidies because poor people lack purchasing power. But I argued that telephones make people more productive and, in turn, give them the necessary purchasing power. I was driven to design a commercial model—with profits as a means, not an end—so that whatever business I succeeded in establishing could sustain itself and expand on its own. It would also demonstrate that poor people needed commercial opportunities, not charity. More important, I was driven to find ways to engage ordinary and poor citizens in commerce, a process through which actual progress can occur, in contrast to large projects pushed by large organizations, which often *dis*engage ordinary citizens and increase poverty.

With these beliefs, I was drawn to Grameen Bank in Bangladesh, which provides small loans to poor people and engages them in tiny commercial projects (e.g., taking care of a cow and selling milk) that generated income for them. My study of the bank led me to conceive of an effective way of distributing telephone services. Borrowers of the bank could use loans to purchase handsets and retail telephone services in their communities. It would create both self-employment opportunities and connectivity.

I moved back to Bangladesh in 1994 to start persuading Grameen Bank to participate in this effort and to search globally for telephone companies and funding sources to join the project, which later became known as GrameenPhone. With seed funds from individual investors in America, I was eventually able to organize a consortium involving eight different organizations from many parts of the world, including the Norwegian telephone company Telenor and Grameen Bank. I needed to build a large network to achieve economies of scale, allowing it to serve many people at low costs. The total investment is now approaching $300 million (starting with $120 million in 1997), with additional funds coming from the company's own profits. With nearly 800,000 subscribers, revenues reached $150 million in 2002.

GrameenPhone's rural program is already available in more than 25,000 villages, providing telephone access to 40 million people. It also means that there are 25,000 microentrepreneurs who, on average, net $2 per day, an amount that is twice the per capita income of the country.

Even though this project appears to be a contemporary technical solution, it actually emerged from a historical perspective for which I owe much to Swarthmore. The school freed my mind so that I was no longer overwhelmed by technical solutions per se or by projects pushed by the strong but rather could keep my eyes on the human priorities that I had learned about from rural Bangladesh and from my father.

&

Iqbal Quadir, whose special interest is the democratizing effects of technologies in developing countries, teaches at Harvard's John F. Kennedy School of Government.

The Unity of
Human Knowledge

Christopher Chyba '82

I entered Swarthmore in the fall of 1977 and, through luck and the advice of upperclassmen, I found myself in Richie Schuldenfrei's Introduction to Philosophy, Jim Kurth's Political Science course, and John Boccio and Jim England's combined Advanced Physics and Math sequence. Quite a first semester! I was impressed by teachers who had thought hard about the world and were trying to live according to what they had decided. I remember walking home late one night from working on what felt like a totally cool assignment—I was computing and plotting the trajectory of a spacecraft transferring from Earth orbit to lunar orbit, in the days before personal computers—and watching the snow fall on me through the illuminated limbs of some of the pines, and being aware of how happy I was, how this was what I had imagined college could turn out to be if everything somehow went right.

Swarthmore is a college, not a university, yet it exemplifies the ideal of the university far better than many universities, whose inertial forces too often drive them to become multiversities, or polyversities. At Swarthmore, the ideal of the unity of human knowledge takes on concrete expression, and not

The College showed me that it was possible—
even desirable—to do more than one thing.

just in course work. I remember Physics Professor (now Congressman) Rush Holt holding his weekly evening Physics in Public Policy seminars in his living room—no course credit offered—and getting an enthusiastic turnout of busy students and faculty from several departments. I remember reading *After Virtue* and *Knowledge and Politics* not because they were assigned in any of my courses, but because my friends were talking about them over dinner and I wanted to take part in the conversation. And I remember Jim Kurth, even after I was no longer in his class, once kicking me in the pants for getting so wrapped up in my science that I was paying too little attention to other issues. And for someone who had not often ventured beyond Baltimore while growing up, Swarthmore taught me great respect for the power and freedom that knowledge of other languages can bring.

Swarthmore gave me the rigor and training I needed to start out pursuing theoretical physics and philosophy, and the flexibility to switch to planetary science and astrobiology when those fields captured my imagination. It helped me gain the breadth I needed to work with Carl Sagan for a Ph.D. in astronomy and the confidence I needed to keep up with him as he roamed across the intellectual landscape. In John Boccio, Swarthmore gave me a scientific mentor whom I paired with Carl in my mind as having helped me learn how to think hard and deep about scientific questions.

The academy's tendency toward specialization and fragmentation pressures students and faculty to stovepipe their interests (and perhaps to create new verbs). Swarthmore helped me to avoid that track. In the mid-1990s, not long after completing my doctoral work, I was fortunate to spend two years serving on the national security staff at the White House. When I left the government and interviewed for my first tenure-track science faculty position, one senior faculty member made clear his opinion of my diversion from academic specialization: "Convince me, Dr. Chyba, that you are not merely broad and shallow." No faculty member at Swarthmore would have asked that question. I think that people at Swarthmore get it in a way that is less common at other schools.

I am fortunate now to belong to two excellent organizations, the SETI Institute and Stanford University, where resistance to intellectual stovepiping is tangibly encouraged and where the divorce of science from the world is discouraged. I now teach undergrads and supervise grad students in researching the exploration of space and the possibilities for life elsewhere, and I also co-direct the Center for International Security and Cooperation (CISAC) in Stanford's Institute for International Studies. Within CISAC, more than 60 scholars pursue policy-relevant research on a range of "post-Cold War" topics, from understanding and diminishing the threat of ethnic violence or the proliferation of nuclear weapons to lessening the effects of mass-casualty terrorism. To whatever extent I am "getting away" with both doing scientific research and working in international security, the stage for this kind of dual career was set for me at Swarthmore. The College showed me that it was possible—even desirable—to do more than one thing and that I could indeed pursue such combinations. It was my great good fortune to have lived and studied there.

Christopher Chyba co-directs the Center for International Security and Cooperation at Stanford University and holds the Carl Sagan Chair for the Study of Life in the Universe at the SETI Institute in Mountain View, Calif.

A Second Chance

Maurice Foley '82

In the fall of 1978, I walked around the campus wearing green army fatigues, shoulder holster, green bandana headscarf, dark sunglasses, and a saunter imbued with an I-wish-you-would-say-something-out-of-line threat. Primed for the streets of Oakland or Philly, I was a little "hard" for the manicured, idyllic, and—to my way of thinking—preppy confines of Swarthmore College. Before my arrival, I had read only one book cover to cover, *The Autobiography of Malcolm X*, by Alex Haley. Though extremely confident in my ability, I was not academically, mentally, or spiritually prepared for what I was about to face: an intense, rigorous academic experience in a somewhat surreal—and certainly foreign—setting.

From the outset, my study habits were poor, and, for the first time, I experienced academic difficulties. Undaunted, I proceeded to endear myself to my fellow students. I started by evicting my roommate for the unpardonable trespass of playing my stereo. During Thanksgiving break, I stole a stereo from a classmate who lived down the hall. In early December, Swarthmore's security officers caught me stealing calculators from the science library. After a feeble attempt to lie my way out of this predicament, I was urged by my older brother to "tell the whole truth and deal with the consequences." I did. First, I told school officials about the transgressions and returned many of the stolen articles. Then I had a difficult conversation with the student whose stereo I had stolen. Finally, I had a hearing before the Student Judicial Council. On Dec. 16, I received the following letter:

> *I regret to inform you that the Committee has decided that the offenses committed by you warrant a one-semester non-notational suspension. It is hoped that the time away from Swarthmore will allow you to evaluate your actions and consider your commitments to Swarthmore. The Committee hopes that you will return in the fall better able to handle the pressures here and by extension better able to control your actions.*

I certainly did not know that my next appearance in a judicial setting would be 17 years later, and I would be the judge. Yet there were many lessons to be learned before I reached that point.

After returning to Swarthmore, I met two people who changed my life. In the fall of 1979, I took African American history with Professor Kathryn Morgan. I remember her entrance on the first day of class—the African garb, short Afro, and large dangling earrings. Professor Morgan was a bona fide soul sista—earthy, militant, fiery, uncompromising, and direct. Radical yet reasoned. Oscillating between a cool, calm, aloof philosopher and an in-your-face "Burn, baby, burn" crusader, she made it clear to the students that it was not appropriate to open your mouth unless you had something substantive to say—leave your rhetoric in a receptacle outside the door. I knew I was going to learn a lot from her, and I did.

After I had taken four of her classes, we developed a new

seminar: Special Topics in Black Studies. It comprised one student from each of seven areas of study–political science, economics, psychology, sociology, anthropology, biology, and history. Each student taught a session explaining how to foster African American social and economic advancement by modifying and employing traditional theories in his or her academic discipline. Professor Morgan's passion for reforming "the system" infused in me a passion for political, economic, and tax matters relevant to African Americans. As a result, during the course of my career in the legislative realm, I particularly enjoyed developing expertise and designing legislation relating to the earned-income tax credit, low-income housing credit, empowerment zones, and other provisions that would significantly affect African Americans.

In the fall of 1980, I met another professor who changed my life and today is one of my closest friends: Richard Rubin. Professor Rubin, like Professor Morgan, was brutally honest with me. During an office visit, he disclosed that he had been a successful businessman before joining academia. I told him that I had my sights set on achieving success in the business world and wanted to know what I needed to do to prepare myself. He was practical, earnest, and wise. He first told me I had to improve my writing skills. Get rid of all the "hearts and flowers"—the fluff—and get to the point. He destroyed my papers and then performed the laborious task of teaching me how to write. His advice and instructions served me well, for I would later be called on to draft complex tax regulations and tax legislation; memos for the secretary of the treasury, chairman of the Senate Finance Committee, and president of the United States; and U.S. Tax Court opinions. There was certainly no room for hearts and flowers.

He then told me that I needed to be "bilingual" and improve my speaking skills in order to succeed in a business world controlled predominantly by whites. In essence, I needed to be more polished. Although I had been a successful

> *I could have been expelled or confronted with criminal charges.*

debater and extemporaneous speaker in high school, I understood what he was telling me. In fact, for most of my childhood, I had had a severe stuttering problem, which I worked on and eventually overcame. Additional fine-tuning of my speech would not be a problem. That summer, I took a public-speaking course.

Finally, he told me that my heart had to change and I had to trust people. I was raised in a military family that moved every couple of years. We lived in obscure places such as Utah and North Dakota. I did not know my aunts, uncles, cousins, or even my grandparents. I made and broke relationships easily and indiscriminately. I was quite comfortable in solitude. In essence, I grew up loving and caring about only my parents, my four siblings, and myself. I had expanded that inner circle to include Cassandra Green '79. (She was the one wise decision mixed in with the many errors of judgment during my first semester. I pursued Cassandra, a Swarthmore senior, with great fervor. She became my best friend and, ultimately, my wife and the loving mother of our three children.) But Professor Rubin pushed me to expand it further—much further. His credo was and continues to be:

> *If I am not for myself, who will be for me?*
> *If I am only for myself, what am I?*
> *If not now, when?*
> *—Pirkei Avot (Ethics of Our Fathers), 1:14, Hillel*

I had no problem being "for myself," but the rest of the quote was a problem. Professor Rubin, however, set the perfect example for why it is important not to be "for myself" and not to delay in helping others. A list of all the insights, advice, and gifts he has given me, my family, and other students might lead you to question his sanity; so, for the purposes of this essay, I will add only that he taught the Macroeconomic Policy course that convinced me to pursue a career in tax law, made sure that I took the requisite prep courses for the LSAT and GMAT, and has provided me with advice regarding all my career decisions.

When I made a mistake at Swarthmore, I did not receive what I deserved. Instead, by God's grace, I received what I did not deserve. I could have been expelled or confronted with criminal charges. Yet I was given a second chance. This experience indelibly seared into my conscience the importance of honesty and integrity, and of directly confronting the consequences of mistakes.

At Swarthmore, I was blessed with two amazing professors and friends who taught me life lessons that guided my personal and professional life. Indeed, today there is a little bit of Rubin and Morgan in every judicial opinion I write. Professor Rubin forged the template long ago with his admonitions to be practical and excise the "hearts and flowers." My opinions also reflect the resolute and direct approach of Professor Morgan. I pray that my legacy, like theirs, will be one of teaching, mentoring, and self-sacrifice for the benefit of others.

᪥

Maurice Foley, a judge on the U.S. Tax Court since 1995, previously served as counsel to the Department of Treasury and the U.S. Senate Committee on Finance.

What Jazz
Teaches Us

Ken Schaphorst '82

Was it while I was sitting in a
quantum mechanics class during my sophomore year, scrib-
bling a musical staff into the margin of my notebook? Or was
it while I was making music with some of the many serious
musicians that I met at Swarthmore? Or was it toward the end
of my sophomore year, when Professor Thomas Oboe Lee
encouraged me to write an ambitious double concerto for
jazz chamber orchestra, which was played by a group of
Swarthmore undergraduates in Lang Concert Hall? All I
know for certain is that when I arrived at Swarthmore
College in the fall of 1978, I had no idea that I would end up
majoring in music, but, by the fall of 1980, when I started my
junior year, I was a music major.

Granted, I had played the piano since I was 6 and started
playing the trumpet when I was 9. In junior high school, I
started composing music, and, by the end of high school, I had
become obsessed with jazz. But when I entered Swarthmore
College, I had no plans to pursue a career in music. I wasn't
sure what I wanted to study, but music was not even under
consideration. At the end of my sophomore year, I was prepar-
ing to return in the fall with a major in economics and a

minor in English literature. Yet over the summer, I realized that music meant more to me than anything else, and I changed my plans. Now that I've spent the past 12 years advising undergraduates, it seems remarkable that I was able to start work on a music major in my junior year and still graduate with my class in 1982. In retrospect, I appreciate Swarthmore's flexibility in allowing me to pursue my rediscovered passion for music so late in the game. But there was more to it than the College's being flexible enough to allow me to take second- and third-year theory at the same time. I'm grateful to Swarthmore for being the kind of place where I could explore so many different disciplines and, through that exploration, discover the course of study that had the greatest meaning for me.

It seems difficult to imagine now, but at various times I also seriously considered majoring in engineering, physics, and classics. I imagine that most Swarthmore students enter with some questions regarding their ultimate course of study, but, looking back on it, I'm tempted to say that I was probably one of the most confused undergraduates around. I now realize that by exploring so many different courses, I was able to learn about many absorbing, stimulating fields of inquiry and, at the same time, see more and more clearly how my passion for music stood out in contrast. I appreciate Swarthmore's patience with this process of self-discovery. I don't know of any other college where this process of finding oneself is such an integral part of the institution's mission.

For the past 12 years, I've been teaching in a conservatory where most of the students are pursuing bachelor of music degrees. Between 1991 and 2001, I directed the jazz program at Lawrence University, a liberal arts college and conservatory in Appleton, Wis. And in 2001, I was appointed chair of the Jazz Studies and Improvisation Department at the New England Conservatory in Boston. During that time, I've often wondered how my life might have been different if I had gone

> *The best music presents a model of human interaction, a template of the human experience.*

to a music conservatory instead of a liberal arts college.

I'll never know, but I have trouble imagining my life without Allan Blair's quantum mechanics class; Tom Bradley's Russian novel course; or Phil Weinstein's Proust, Joyce, and Faulkner. Having an intellectual life outside of music has certainly helped me along the way. My Swarthmore education helped me in 1985, when I was setting up the Jazz Composers Alliance, a nonprofit corporation dedicated to new music in the jazz idiom, which is still active. It has also helped me in my academic work, where the ability to think and write clearly has proved to be more critical than I could possibly have imagined. But most important, it opened me up to a world of ideas that influences me every day.

It's the combination of a serious study of music and broad intellectual pursuits that has been the most meaningful aspect of my Swarthmore education. While teaching musicians, I'm always aware that I'm teaching more than just music, more than just how to compose or perform. The best music presents a model of human interaction, a template of the human experience. A Mozart string quartet represents a model of mutual respect, cooperation, and harmony that we would all do well to emulate. A jazz ensemble presents a model of how such a strikingly dissimilar group of instruments as piano, bass, and drums can find a common language and communicate profound ideas through that language. If people could behave the way musicians interact with one another in the best music making, the world would be a better place.

My Swarthmore education has also helped me understand and articulate the meaning of jazz. By reflecting the society in which it developed, jazz can teach us about that society and express its truths to us through music. Jazz teaches us to respect each individual's voice. Jazz teaches us the importance of attentive listening. Jazz represents one of the most compelling examples of the natural dance of soul and intellect.

Swarthmore has shaped me in ways I cannot fully comprehend, much less put into words. It was there that I met my wife, Ellen Argyros '83; we were married in the College's amphitheater on a beautiful summer day in 1989. But perhaps Swarthmore's greatest gift was the patience and loving support granted to me at a time when I needed it the most.

⊹⊹⊹

Ken Schaphorst, chair of the Jazz Studies and Improvisation Department at the New England Conservatory of Music, is also a founder and member of the Boston-based Jazz Composers Alliance and leader of the Ken Schaphorst Big Band.

We Are All
Connected

Laura Markowitz '85

My very first class at Swarthmore
was called Buddhist Ethics in Contemporary Perspective. I
didn't know much about Buddhism, but I had been drawn to
the course by the description of the professor in the catalog:
Dr. Gunapala Dharmasiri, Lang Visiting Professor, a Buddhist
philosopher from Sri Lanka. At age 17, my goal for my college
education was to discover the meaning of life, and I thought a
philosopher-professor would have interesting ideas on that
topic. I was right.

I remember how he looked that first day. He was perched
on the edge of a desk, a small man with enormous eyes. Over
the next few classes, he patiently explained the concepts of
karma, rebirth, the Four Noble Truths, and the Eightfold Path.
I was immediately drawn to the dharma, the teachings of the
Buddha. When I wasn't analyzing *The Heart of Darkness* in
Craig Williamson's freshman English class or arguing Marxist
theory in the History Department, I thought about the
Buddha's philosophy. I agreed with the First Noble Truth, that
life is suffering. But what was the best course of action to take
to avoid suffering?

Buddha taught that our belief in a Self was what caused

us to suffer. This was the most difficult concept to grasp. I argued that if there was no Self, who was supposed to read the assignment for next week's class? Dharme, as I came to know him, explained that we really exist on two levels: the worldly, everyday life we think of as reality is actually based on this illusion of an immutable Me, a Self; there was another level, which he called Ultimate Reality, which was the true nature of things. Ultimate Reality was right here, right now; we just didn't comprehend it yet, so we continued to paddle around on the level of illusion.

One day, we discussed ethics. How did Buddhists understand right and wrong? "When one is truly enlightened, one understands implicitly that all beings are connected," Dharme told us. "And so, doing harm becomes impossible. It would be like cutting off one's own arm to harm another being." A senior in the class challenged Dharme, saying that the Buddha taught that the only way to understand Ultimate Reality was to withdraw from the world and become a monk or nun, but wasn't that unethical? If we were all connected, didn't each of us have a responsibility to redress social wrongs? Should spiritual seekers just turn their backs on social justice and do nothing but pursue their own enlightenment?

Dharme agreed that it was selfish to coast off into the bliss of Nirvana without considering the suffering of those left behind. He pointed out that the Buddha himself made a conscious decision to stay in the world and become a teacher of the dharma, so he could help others attain liberation from suffering.

I was impressed by the great compassion implicit in this. That week, inspired to be helpful, I joined the Swarthmore Anti-Apartheid Social Action Committee. We met in a small study room on the second floor of Tarble, two years before it burned down. The two seniors were appalled at how little I knew about the situation in South Africa. They gave me books about Biko and Mandela and the African National Congress.

We circulated a petition to get the College to divest itself of its South African holdings in protest of the racist government. I started to read about racism here in the United States and began to notice how white Swarthmore looked and how segregated my own life had been. I also joined the Women's Center and started to learn more about the systemic oppression of women around the world and developed a language for articulating my own experiences of sexism.

The influence of Dharme's lessons are clearer to me now than they were then: While I was learning about patriarchy, dominance and oppression, discrimination, and other human atrocities, I could never pretend it had nothing to do with me. It was clear that although I was a victim in one context, I was someone else's oppressor in another. Dharme's profound statement that all beings are connected has stayed with me through my career. When I write about differences, I am also aware that we are not, ultimately, different from one another. Being a journalist has given me opportunities to shift the discourse from either/or, us/them dichotomies and to invite new ways of understanding. The seemingly simple statement that we are all connected on the most fundamental level opens up rich possibilities. It means we always have a choice. We always have the potential to be compassionate and help others.

The second semester of my sophomore year, I went off to Sri Lanka to study with Dharme, and he generously invited me to stay with his family. I took classes in Buddhist philosophy, and also Western philosophy and psychology from a Buddhist perspective. After a few months, my visa ran out, and I ended up in Thailand; practiced Vipassana meditation in a monastery; and, when that visa expired a few months later, I went on a Buddhist pilgrimage to Burma, Nepal, and India.

I spent a lot of time grappling with the disjunction between the beautiful philosophy of Buddhism and the obvious sexism of the religious institution. In Thailand, for example, a monk could not even accept a piece of paper from a

I argued that if there was no Self, who was supposed to read the assignment for next week's class?

woman's hand, for fear of contamination. I tried to be respectful, but I found it infuriating. And in Sri Lanka, there was a kind of caste system among the orders of monks, based on class. I had to wrestle with my disappointment that institutionalized Buddhism had its failings. Dharme had his criticisms too, but he was doing something about it: translating Buddhist texts into Sinhalese and later founding an educational organization for Buddhist nuns. His quiet social activism inspired me, years later, to start a magazine for lesbian, gay, bisexual, and transgender families. I knew a nonmainstream publication would probably never become a great financial success or win me prestigious awards and that, as a journalist, I might be stigmatized for covering an unpopular topic. But I saw there was something I could do to help alternative families thrive, and I heard Dharme's advice in my head: "It's good to be a small fry!"

When I returned to Swarthmore, I experienced culture shock. Had McCabe Library shrunk? Was Sharples always so noisy? It was difficult to keep up my eight-hours-a-day meditation regimen. I lived on the third floor of Parrish, in a single overlooking the rose garden, and I sat on the generous window sill and read Virginia Woolf and struggled with cellular and molecular biology. The famous suffragette Alice Paul, for whom our Women's Center was named, had lived in my room. It was going to be her centennial that year, and our group was planning events to commemorate it. While I had been gone, there had been discussions about the fact that the "Women's Center" was almost completely a "white women's center." We talked a lot about why "they" weren't coming to "our" meetings. Alice Paul's decision not to support suffrage for African American women made us uncomfortable. How could we celebrate her achievement but also acknowledge this terrible omission? We decided to address it by inviting an African American civil rights lawyer to be our keynote speaker. Dr. Mary Frances Berry was an impressive activist, and we hoped her talk would create a bridge with our African American sisters at Swarthmore. But the night of Dr. Berry's talk, the audience was almost wholly white. It turned out we had scheduled the talk on a night when the Black Cultural Center had scheduled its own special event.

I had volunteered to drive Dr. Berry back to the airport; in the car, I asked her advice. What could we do to be more inclusive? She suggested we listen to African American women on campus. "You need to find out what you have in common and where you can work in coalition. Let trust build from that collaboration." My senior year, in Kathryn Morgan's Oral History class, I learned this lesson again: If you want to connect with people, you have to respect them. You have to be genuine and curious, and you have to listen. As a journalist, I find value in those lessons over and over again.

Another profound teacher of this lesson was also a woman of color. Fatima Meer came from South Africa to be a Lang Visiting Professor for the spring semester of my junior year. She had problems getting permission from her government to leave the country because of her jail record. She'd been imprisoned for anti-apartheid activism. My best friend, Robin Moore, was a family friend of Fatima's, and he brought me to see her one night soon after she arrived. I immediately loved her. She was an energetic whirlwind who would suddenly pause and let loose the most wonderful smile. She had a constant stream of company; people came from all over the country to meet with her. I started coming to her house regularly to wash the dishes that piled up in her sink. I had a car and took her to the store to buy groceries.

I had just come out, and I was shy to speak of it, but I think she knew. We cooked food and sat in her living room and talked about feminism, religion, politics, her life. We often disagreed, but she had a way of never getting defensive. She made room at the table for divergent viewpoints and respected our differences. She showed me how listening with an open mind and heart can build a bridge. I admired her intrepid spirit. "You have to stand up to injustice, no matter how small," she advised me during an outing to the grocery store. I accidentally turned into the parking lot's exit lane. "Never mind," she told me. "Just proceed! Never lose confidence! Never lose confidence about doing the right thing! Just proceed!" I lost contact with Fatima after she returned to South Africa. But I hear her words in my head all the time: "Just proceed!" Do what you know is right, and trust that it will all work out for the best.

I recently found this advice in a book of Buddhist quotations: "If for company you find a wise and prudent friend who leads a good life, you should, overcoming all impediments, keep his [or her] company joyously and mindfully." I e-mailed it to Dharme with a note: "I can never thank you enough for teaching me about Buddhism and for your friendship." For the past two decades, Dharme has been one of my closest friends and confidants. He wrote back this morning: "Thanks so much for the beautiful words of inspiration. It makes the whole life so meaningful."

Laura Markowitz, a writer and editor, is the founder and publisher of the magazine In the Family.

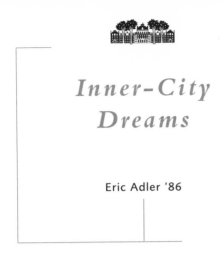

Inner-City
Dreams

Eric Adler '86

My high school taught me
what a preparatory education should be. My graduate school
gave me the skills to build a business to deliver that education
to poor children. But Swarthmore taught me why I should
devote my life to such a project. Like so many of us, I became
who I am at Swarthmore.

In my senior year, I wrote two theses: my Engineering
090 project and an economics thesis titled "The Causes of
Economic Inequity in America." While my friends at other
colleges were breezing through their final semesters, I must
have pulled a dozen all-nighters in a four-month period. I
found myself engrossed in the study of how various groups
have fared economically in America and elsewhere, and what
problems stood between them and economic justice. Fifteen
years later, I am working full time on a project designed
specifically to address the issues I studied in my thesis. Here is
how I got here:

Swarthmore and its Quaker values have played a critical
role in my life. I attended not only a Quaker college but also
a Quaker high school. I am married to the most wonderful
Quaker on earth, Suzanne Myers Adler '97. (Score another

one for the Quaker Matchbox!) Suzanne's maid of honor and the godmother of our daughter is Nora Taylor '97, also a Quaker. In my junior year, Will Saletan '87 invited me to join his radio comedy show, *Swarthmore Adult Movie Theatre*. We did sketches and political satire. We thought we were the funniest thing in the entire world. Today, we hear the tapes and realize that we weren't really all that funny at all. But Will lives just a few miles from me and is our daughter's godfather. It turns out that being funny isn't the most important part of doing a radio comedy program in college.

I grew up in a middle-class home, played lots of soccer, and fooled around with various mechanical and electrical devices and science kits. I happily attended suburban public schools through the eighth grade and then moved to Sidwell Friends, a well-known Quaker high school in Washington, D.C. My experience there impressed me deeply; I realized that the quality of one's education could make or break a life.

I arrived at Swarthmore determined to develop my interest in mechanics and electronics, and majored in engineering and economics. I knew that the first thing I wanted to do after graduation was to teach high school. I wanted to help provide to others the very successful high school experience I had enjoyed.

My first job after Swarthmore was teaching high school physics at St. Paul's School in Baltimore. I loved my time there and stayed for eight years, eventually becoming dean of students. But I had an entrepreneurial itch that I needed to scratch. So, in 1994, I headed to the Wharton School to earn an M.B.A. I received the phone call from Lisa Lee—yes, *our* Lisa Lee, Swarthmore Class of '81 and now director of alumni relations, who was a member of the Wharton School admissions staff back then—informing me that I had been admitted to Wharton. I remember thinking that the only way I could have gotten in, with my college grades, was if there was a Swarthmorean on the admissions staff!

After Wharton, I took a job as a management consultant. However, helping enormous corporations to operate a little more efficiently, although honorable work, just did not seem as important as teaching. And yet, I had these business skills, and I wanted to put them to work toward a greater good, so I decided to start a social venture. Because I believe that education is the answer to nearly every social ill and that social problems are concentrated in our inner cities, I decided to build schools for the inner city. I realized that college-preparatory boarding schools for inner-city children, most of whom would be statistically expected to drop out of school, could prepare them instead for admission to America's most competitive colleges and universities.

Six years ago, my business partner, Raj Vinnakota, and I launched the SEED (Schools for Educational Evolution and Development) Foundation, whose mission is to open and operate such schools. Five years ago, we opened our first school, right here in my hometown of Washington, D.C., which serves as a model for others we intend to open, perhaps all across the country. The SEED School of Washington, the nation's only public college-preparatory boarding school, is located within the urban neighborhood from which many of its students are drawn. In these five years, we have seen inner-city children grow from immature preteens to secure and self-disciplined young men and women. Next year, we will send the first couple of dozen of them off to college. And these students were not creamed off as the most promising among thousands from the inner city; we accept applications from any poor children who want to attend, and choose our students by lottery. The SEED School is proving that inner-city children, no matter how difficult their circumstances, can be prepared for their rightful share of the American dream, if we only care enough to do it.

The process has been grueling. Raj and I have worked many 100-hour weeks. We have raised nearly $35 million in capital, more than $20 million of which has come through cash gifts and the rest through tax-exempt bonds. We still have millions of dollars left to raise. We have successfully lobbied the federal and D.C. governments for $7.3 million of annual operating funding and have developed 175,000 square feet of finished space in four buildings on the school's 19-acre campus. As you read these words, we have 300 students living and learning and eating and sleeping on our campus, becoming who they want to become.

We have been treated generously by donors, by our incredibly committed faculty and staff, and by the press. The recognition we have received has been beyond my wildest imaginings: The SEED School has been featured on broadcasts such as *ABC News Nightline* and the PBS documentary program *Life 360*. Raj and I were honored to receive the Use Your Life Award on the Oprah Winfrey Show. (The next day I received a call from a woman in California who said: "I saw you on Oprah yesterday. My house is on the market, and I am coming to work for you." And she did!) Recently, Raj and I were named "2002 Washingtonians of the Year" by *The Washingtonian* magazine. We have also been named fellows by the Echoing Green Foundation and have received the Manhattan Institute's Outstanding Social Entrepreneur Award. Most surprising of all, the cover of a recent *Wharton Alumni Magazine* featured not some corporate raider or Internet mogul, but a social entrepreneur who builds schools.

What is it about Swarthmore that changed me, and helped me become the social entrepreneur that I am today? First and foremost, it was the focus on academics. Swarthmore allowed me to see that concentrating on the life of the mind is important. Second, it was the lack of grade inflation (or, perhaps, the existence of grade *deflation*!). In a world all too accepting of poor quality, it is exciting to have been nurtured by a place that calls mediocrity to account. Swarthmore helped me to see that if I am to accomplish anything important in life, it will

It is exciting to have been nurtured by a place that calls mediocrity to account.

not be by coasting.

But the other extraordinary influence that Swarthmore had on me was to surround me with kind role models. I remember as a student once reading an interview with a young alum who said, "It took me a couple of years after Swarthmore to realize that the rest of the world really *is* out to get me." I particularly remember Curt Lauber (the varsity soccer coach), Fred Orthlieb (my Engineering 090 adviser), and Paul Rabideau (my economics thesis adviser), each treating me with great kindness and respect, despite moments in which they could have cut me to shreds. Kenneth Gergen and Kaori Kitao handled me with kid gloves when I made the mistakes of enrolling in social psychology and art history courses I had no business attempting. Coming of age in a place devoted to kindness and decency is a precious gift.

Even Eugene Lang '38, one of Swarthmore's most generous donors and, at the time of my graduation, chairman of the Board of Managers, treated me with incredible kindness. The day before I graduated, he granted me a meeting after a cold call, without knowing what I wanted. In fact, I didn't know what I wanted either, beyond the fact that this man was a stunningly successful entrepreneur who worked with technology, and I just knew that he was the sort of person I should meet. And so I did. Fifteen years later, he would grant me a second meeting to discuss the SEED Foundation and allow me to try to interest him in supporting it. In the end, he declined, but in turning me down, he offered some of the kindest words of encouragement I have ever received. In that moment, Eugene Lang showed me the difference between not supporting and not caring.

I carry Swarthmore's lessons about kindness, hard work, and academic study with me to this day. They affect me not only as a social leader, but as a husband, father, and friend. All of us who graduated from Swarthmore are lucky to have had the experience of attending a special little college. To the extent that we are able to accomplish good works, the whole world is lucky that we went to Swarthmore.

Eric Adler is co-founder and executive director of the SEED Foundation, which creates college-preparatory schools for inner-city children.

You Can Get
There from Here

Barbara Klock '86

I entered Swarthmore College long after the concept of student diversity became ingrained in the campus lingo but shortly before the concept of multiculturalism took hold. As a fair-haired, fair-skinned female, I surely did not appear to diversify the campus, but I did. During orientation week, I enthusiastically tapped on a Willets door and greeted my new hallmate with my Philadelphia accent. He responded, "You talk funny."

Before coming to Swarthmore, I had never known teenagers whose parents had Ph.D.s. I had never used the words "middle class" or "working class" in casual conversation—I didn't know that people compartmentalized the world that way. I remember saying to someone, while strolling back to Willets during my freshman year, "The working class can't stop to analyze their plight because they're too busy living it."

My life had always been about service. As a high school student in Philadelphia, I had organized numerous community-service initiatives with Cambodian refugees, homeless children, and others. During freshman year, a professor said to me, "I'm not used to someone from your background being so involved in social service." I didn't know that certain back-

As a fair-haired, fair-skinned female, I surely did not appear to diversify the campus, but I did.

grounds made you feel more or less committed to helping someone live a little better.

My life at Swarthmore continued to be about service and children; therefore, the Education Program was the perfect haven for me. Bob Gross '62, Eva Travers, Ann Renninger, and Lisa Smulyan '76 patiently taught me to be a better writer, a thorough thinker—and a focused activist. When I met with Eva Travers to discuss my vision for my Lang Community Service Project, I wanted to teach kids about racism, women's issues, the rights of the disabled, and every other social injustice. In her nurturing way, she helped me mold my vision into a focused, manageable, and effective form. She taught me to choose one thing and do it well. I call on that experience frequently when planning things today.

During my time at Swarthmore, I probably spent one too many Saturdays scraping paint off abandoned houses in Chester or ducking under the lilacs with faculty kids I was baby-sitting when I should have been completing my reading in McCabe Library. As a consequence, what I remember most about Swarthmore today is the people. When I go back there and Bob Gross greets me with a hug, memories of Introduction to Education in the Cloisters flash in front of me—flashes of laughter and a listening ear and a circle of students working together, cultivated by Bob's open and warm manner. I love it when my former professors come up to me and tell me about their grown children whom I pushed through Parrish Hall in strollers. Although I may not have had classes with these professors, I was part of their experience of juggling the raising of young children with the building of a career. As was the case before I came to Swarthmore, I still consider myself much more of a doer than a thinker, but the people who influenced me at Swarthmore prepared me to question why things are the way they are and educated me to be confident that I can effect change.

While at Swarthmore, I was lucky to bridge the worlds of academia and my working-class upbringing. Today, as a pediatrician, I see the benefits of that bridging. Many of the families who come to me are solid working-class Philadelphians. They respect my education and also know I'll deliver news straight from the hip.

Back in 1985, at a College graduation party for a friend, one of his relatives commented: "Interesting. How does someone from Juniata Park [my neighborhood in Philadelphia] get to a place like Swarthmore College?" "Easy," I said. "Route I-95."

⚶

Barbara Klock is a pediatrician at Children's Hospital of Philadelphia.

That Powerful
Sense of Hope

Jennifer Rickard '86

W hen I speak with prospective
Bryn Mawr students about the importance of their college
decisions, I'm reminded of the randomness of my own college
search—and of the unexpected consequences of choosing
Swarthmore. There was something in the easy way that my
acceptance letter from Dean of Admissions Robert Barr Jr. '56
conveyed the importance of Swarthmore's values of intellectual pursuit, tolerance, community—and the use of education
to help others—that made me feel hopeful that I could
accomplish anything in my life. That hope faded a few months
later when a high school classmate told me of my chosen college's nickname, "Sweatmore." During that long summer
before my freshman year, neither my extracurricular nor my
academic accomplishments in high school reassured me that I
was college material.

Having grown up in California's hotbed of intercollegiate
sports competition, I had abandoned any notion of continuing my athletic pursuits in college. After watching high-pow-
ered teams representing such schools as Stanford, UCLA, and
Berkeley, I knew I was not "college" caliber as an athlete. And
since Swarthmore was a "college," I was sure I would not be

playing there. Nevertheless, thanks to the urging of one of my roommates who had arrived early for field hockey, I decided to try out for the basketball team my freshman year. To my surprise, I made the team as a "walk-on."

I learned that there existed a Division III in NCAA athletics. At that time, Division III was about playing on a Swarthmore team with people from New York, Kuwait, North Carolina, Mexico City, California, and Delaware County, Pa., who were engineers, philosophers, biologists, and political scientists who wanted to play basketball simply because they liked it. Sophomore year, when I returned to campus early from winter break for basketball practice, I realized how much being a part of a team meant to me. I was enjoying the heightened athletics challenge of intercollegiate play, but, more important, I was enjoying learning how to balance my life and how to work with others very different from myself. I belonged at Swarthmore.

I remember a similar sense of belonging at Swarthmore while researching a paper in the Cornell Science Library during my junior year. I was a political science major and a denizen of McCabe. What on earth was I doing in Cornell? I was taking a cross-listed religion and physics course called Issues in Arms Control and Disarmament taught by Jerry Frost and Rush Holt, and I was writing a paper on the effectiveness of nuclear-free zones. I was excited about the opportunity to do research on both the politics and the science behind nuclear proliferation and about the fact that, for the first time at Swarthmore, I felt a sense of mastery not only over how to do the research but how to frame my analysis. I definitely belonged at Swarthmore.

As dean of admissions and financial aid at Bryn Mawr College, I talk about the value of a liberal arts education on a daily basis. My Swarthmore education taught me how to analyze; how to write; how to research; how to solve problems; and how to support my arguments as a humanist, a social sci-

I realized how much being part of a team meant to me.

entist, and a scientist. That academic foundation, when combined with my equally influential extracurricular experiences, has enabled me to work as, successively, a financial accountant, a college admissions officer, a systems-implementation consultant, a software developer, a business executive, and now a college administrator. It has also enabled me to see how all of these seemingly different roles are interrelated. What I found at Swarthmore was more than rigor. I also found hope.

So how did any of this lead to what I call my obsession with college admissions? I think it has something to do with the fact that through my experiences at Swarthmore, I developed that sense of hopefulness. At age 18, I entered Swarthmore an idealistic and intellectually undeveloped young woman. I graduated from Swarthmore still idealistic but intellectually prepared. Added to that idealism was a sense of hope that I really could make a difference in the world and that communities with the values of tolerance and mutual respect really could exist. I am truly grateful to Swarthmore for giving me that powerful sense of hope. It has empowered me to aspire to and accomplish things I would never have thought were within my reach—from playing NCAA basketball to feeling confidence in my intellectual ability. And I think that is why I do what I do now.

Every day, I have the opportunity to expose young women to a community very similar to the one I experienced at Swarthmore. They come to us at a time in their lives when they have no idea what lies ahead for them, and they have no idea what impact college will have on their lives. All they can see is an admissions world fraught with rankings, test scores, media hype, and information overload that often obscure the core of what college is really all about. In my own way, I'm here to give them hope.

Jennifer Rickard is dean of admissions and financial aid at Bryn Mawr College.

Questioning Authority

William Saletan '87

My freshman year, I fell in love with philosophy. My roommate and I had it all figured out: He was going to be a journalist, and I was going to be a philosopher. Twenty years later, he's a philosopher, and I'm a journalist. But philosophy never took the journalist out of him, and journalism never took the philosopher out of me. I'm just teaching and learning in a different place. My classroom is the Internet. My syllabus is current events.

My first job out of college was at *The Hotline*, an electronic political digest, in 1987. The World Wide Web didn't exist. Newspapers uploaded their political stories to us overnight, and we condensed them into a downloadable briefing. I became the editor and found myself in the middle of a presidential campaign, with all the responsibility anyone my age could ask for. But I didn't want to spend my life writing about who was up or down in the polls. I hadn't gone to Swarthmore for a fancy title or invitations to the right cocktail parties. I'd gone there because I thought life had to be more than that.

Swarthmore is the kind of school you choose if you want a really big challenge. Not the superficial challenge of climbing the ladder that's been put in front of you, but the more dif-

> *I hadn't gone to Swarthmore for a fancy title or invitations to the right cocktail parties.*

ficult challenge of figuring out which ladder is worth climbing, or building a ladder to a place no one has imagined before. In 1990, I decided it was time to stop working on other people's projects and start creating my own. I wanted to tackle the sort of questions I'd studied at Swarthmore—questions on which people disagreed not just about means but about ends. So, in 1991, I left my job to write a book about abortion.

Along the way, my politics changed. While doing research and interviews for the book, I was writing articles for *Mother Jones*. The more I read, heard, and wrote, the more out of place I felt on the left. The professors who had influenced me were liberals, but they had given me a liberal education. They had taught me to question authority, even their own. Yes, they had introduced me to Karl Marx. But Marx's lesson wasn't in his delusions of postcapitalist paradise. It was in his ability to see the assumptions of his world from the outside. That's what freed him from the dogmas of capitalism—and freed me and others from the dogmas of Marxism.

In 1996, Michael Kinsley, my former boss, asked me to write for *Slate*, a magazine he was launching on the Internet. The new medium, coupled with Kinsley's adventurous spirit, presented an opportunity to develop new kinds of journalism. I proposed a column called "Frame Game." It would show readers how politicians, pundits, and interest groups manipulated public opinion by framing the issues of the day. When Democrats opposed "spending" federal money on tax cuts, they were obscuring the difference between handouts and earned income. When Republicans preached "judicial restraint," they were concealing their own interpretations of the Constitution.

In writing "Frame Game," I found a synthesis of everything I had learned at Swarthmore: the clarity of philosophy, the nuance of literature, the practicality of political science, and the emancipatory imagination of radical social theory. My job was to expose the assumptions that rigged and circumscribed public debate. Other columnists argued about how to answer the question of the week. "Frame Game" asked how that question had been formulated, by whom, and why. It illuminated the tricks of the left as well as the right. Emancipation is too important to be left to the so-called emancipators.

My book, *Bearing Right*, came out in 2003. It's a case study in framing. It explains how feminists repackaged abortion rights as an antigovernment issue to make it attractive to conservative voters—and how that repackaging led to a libertarian rather than feminist regime of abortion laws. That stuff we heard at Swarthmore about the dialectic of industry and ideology turns out to be more than blather. Interest groups do manufacture ideas. But ideas have dynamics of their own, and sometimes they overpower their creators.

Today, I cover politics in *Slate's* "Ballot Box" column. I still write about framing, but my interest is shifting toward science. The great story of our age isn't in politics. It's in biotechnology. Through cloning, genetic engineering, and the manipulation of body and tissue formation, we're remaking ourselves. We're turning human embryos into human parts and vice versa. We're mixing our DNA with the DNA of other species. Human ingenuity—a synthesis of agriculture, manufacturing, and information technology—is dissolving human nature. I don't know how to answer the moral questions implicit in that revolution, but I do know that they're being hidden and that I'm going to drag them into the open. That isn't where or how I expected to practice philosophy two decades ago. But that's why they call it education.

᧸᧸

William Saletan, chief political correspondent for the on-line magazine Slate, *has also written a book and articles for other publications.*

A Light
That Shines
Very Brightly

Patrick Awuah Jr. '89

W hen I received the invitation
to write about the meaning that Swarthmore has had for me,
I was thrilled because I immediately understood what a wonderful opportunity this was to talk about the College, to
strengthen our fellowship, and to invite others into it. I also
thought this would be an easy essay for me to write. Surely it
should be easy to tell the story of a Ghanaian kid who came
to Swarthmore in 1985 with $50 in his pocket and then expe-
rienced a dramatic transformation in his life. I was wrong. It
has been a struggle to write for an audience that includes my
fellow alumni. I can't imagine anything that I could say here
that hasn't already been said to you. Still, I'll try.

After graduating in 1989 with majors in engineering and
economics, I headed off to work at Microsoft for what I
thought would be a two-year stint that would enable me to
put away money for graduate school. Life turned out very differently from the one I had planned; I stayed at Microsoft for
eight years. In my sixth year, I began to question my assumptions about my purpose in life—and I rediscovered
Swarthmore. My search led me to a somewhat startling conclusion: that I needed to bring the Swarthmore experience

back to Ghana. It took me another two years to leave Microsoft and begin to implement this decision. With tremendous help from faculty at the College, and encouragement and support from President Alfred H. Bloom, a new college called Ashesi University College (named according to conventions used in Ghana) was established in Ghana in 2002.

For me, Ashesi is an expression of the essence of Swarthmore College, which I see as a light that shines very brightly and should shine elsewhere in the world. It is a light that has changed my life in ways I could not imagine when I applied to join this fellowship. And it is a light that continues to shine for me and for everything that I do. Even as I type this essay, Professor Fred Orthlieb, who taught my first engineering class at Swarthmore, is here in Accra co-teaching a design course. Words cannot describe how comforting it is to have Fred here with me.

The purest form of my feelings about Swarthmore can best be found in the way I describe Swarthmore to the Ashesi students. What follows is what I told our most recent incoming class about the meaning of Swarthmore.

> *"We shall not cease from exploration*
> *and the end of all our exploring*
> *will be to arrive where we started*
> *and know the place for the first time*
> —T.S. Eliot

"Class of 2006, *akwaaba!* Welcome to Ashesi University. We are thrilled to have you join our community. We are excited about the new beginning that you represent for us and the new start that our institution represents for you.

"In just 28 words, T.S. Eliot shares with us a profound insight about life's journey. About the need for persistence in our quest and the wisdom that comes from returning to our beginnings—the innocence, the curiosity, and the sense of wonder. As young children, the world seemed a very big place, full of delightful things, and sometimes full of danger. We never hesitated then to ask questions like Why? What? Who? When? How?

"I lost that sense of wonderment during my teenage years, but, at age 20, my college experience rekindled that spirit. Swarthmore College, where I experienced this renewal, is a place that still gives me goose bumps when I visit. It is a place where everyone is allowed, indeed required, to ask: Why? What? Who? When? How?—and to keep asking until they truly understand.

"Ashesi University is my attempt to bring that special spark that I found at Swarthmore back to Ghana. The "starting place"—the beginning—in Eliot's poem can also represent returning home with greater insight and conviction.

"My journey back to Ghana has entailed a few rough bumps, such as a time in 1990 when the difficulties and restrictions I saw during a brief visit home led me to believe that I would never return here to stay. But in May 1995, the birth of my first child created a new reality that helped me grow up.

"Have you ever seen the face of a newborn baby?
Have you ever seen the face of a new mother when
  Baby looks up at her?
Have you ever seen the face of a newborn baby?
It's like seeing the face of God.

"This was my attempt in 1995 to describe my son's birth to my friends. The event of his birth began a period of considerable turmoil for me, as I grappled with the question of how the world would affect him. More precisely, as I looked at my African son, I became increasingly concerned about the state of Africa's economy and society, and the effect it might have on his future. Thus began my quest, with strong support from my wife, Rebecca, to create an institution of higher learning dedicated to training a new generation of ethical,

> *My search led me to a somewhat startling conclusion: that I needed to bring the Swarthmore experience back to Ghana.*

entrepreneurial African leaders. Thankfully, many more people have shared this inspiration with Rebecca and me. With their help, on March 4, 2002, Ashesi University was born.

"Ashesi's first year of instruction was an incredible experience. At times, it almost seemed magical to see the transformation among our students, as Ashesi's pioneers, Class of 2005, rose up to the challenge we presented to them. I am convinced that this year—and indeed your next four years—will be every bit as memorable and rewarding.

"Since our modest beginning last year, our faculty and staff strength has increased considerably, and our student enrollment has also increased in size, quality, and diversity. It is no exaggeration to say that you are among a very select and privileged few who have been chosen to join the Ashesi community. You represent a diverse group of individuals who come from Ethiopia, Ghana, Ivory Coast, Liberia, Nigeria, and Sierra Leone; from east to west; from rural villages to metropolitan cities. Yet you also represent a quite uniform group— a cohort of young adults, each of whom holds great capacity to become a leader.

"Many of you, perhaps all of you, have joined us here at Ashesi with the singular purpose of enhancing your career and economic opportunities. You will get that—and more.

"Here at Ashesi, we seek to nurture the leaders of tomorrow's Africa: leaders with a strong appreciation of their responsibility to society and the strength of character to live up to that responsibility. And we do this by inviting you to come on a quest with us, on an exploration of the world we live in. The education you receive here will teach you how to ask the right questions and will give you the tools to assist in your inquiry for the answers and deeper truths.

"Together, we will discuss the age-old questions about what a good society is, and how best to organize the economic activity of such a society. Here at Ashesi, you will acquire clarity and strength of thinking that will make you the great leaders that you are all so capable of becoming. And, of course, you will be equipped with practical skills in business administration and computer science that will serve you well in your budding careers.

"Today, with all the discord in the world; with the cacophony, the constant drumbeat of war across the globe; with the turmoil in the world's financial and product markets; and in the face of the raging HIV/AIDS epidemic—which continues its deadly march, especially in sub-Saharan Africa—it is more important than ever that we strengthen our resolve to accomplish our mission.

"What we do here is nothing short of a search for the future prosperity, the future dignity, the future happiness of the African people, and, ultimately, of humanity. I know you're up to the task.

"We shall not cease from exploration
and the end of all our exploring
will be to arrive where we started
and know the place for the first time.

"Class of 2006, welcome to this expedition we call Ashesi University. I wish you a very successful and rewarding journey in the years to come."

And so it is that we have embarked on quest to fill Ghana with Swarthmore's light. To my fellow alums, I say: Wish us luck in Ghana, and support your alma mater. This light is worth keeping and worth strengthening.

꧁꧂

Patrick Awuah Jr. is the founder and president of Ashesi
University College in Ghana.

Crises and
Epiphanies

Jonathan Glater '93

The improvisational comedy troupe we enjoyed during my four years of college gave me an analogy for the Swarthmore experience, if not its meaning, of which I am not certain. At the close of one of their performances, members of Vertigo-Go listed some of the skits that they had not performed for us, skits with names but no details. One of them was called *Epiphany Warehouse*.

As far as I know, the skit never was presented, and we never learned what might happen in an epiphany warehouse. But I imagine an experience not unlike college, full of crises and corresponding epiphanies. Trying to finish massive amounts of reading in ridiculously short periods of time without enough sleep created a crisis; realizing that not every word of every assigned reading had to be analyzed for every class was an epiphany—and a critical one at that. This discovery saved me from death by lack of sleep during my first semester, the one that was graded pass/fail.

Crisis may be too strong a word, it seems to me now. When I was a student, though, every challenge, no matter how small, really was a crisis. Every solution really did seem to call for an epiphany. Everything was a mountainous molehill.

At most other schools, very few people would have listened to my concerns, tolerated my memos, or considered the ideas I tried to outline in them.

Today, I know that it was a luxury to treat every minor problem, whether a messy laser-tag feud with a hallmate or an incomprehensible phrase by Shakespeare, with the gravity more appropriate to an earth-shattering concern. And at the same time, I had not only the time but also the obligation to ponder abstract ideas of great import, such as the future ideal structure of society or the nature of merit.

The social possibilities of college created a crisis of the less weighty category. How could I possibly make even a dent in my homework, if I also wanted to battle natural nerd tendencies? The epiphany there came in two stages. First, I came up with a disciplined system, allowing myself to attend many parties but to remain at one for hours and hours only if I spontaneously decided that it was fun; second, I would let that happen only once a semester. It was a good system, except when my one party fell the night before a seminar paper was due.

This sounds overly monastic, even if it did not feel so at the time. Possibly it was, though; I remember my junior year, living on the fourth floor of Parrish in an isolated corner room that had two windows, and two radiators that kept me too warm in the winter. Perhaps I remember that room because it captured, in many ways, how I thought of Swarthmore itself: wonderfully isolated, quiet, spacious. It provided me with the space to think and to learn.

In that junior year, I began to take seminars that met just once a week, and so I had the time to read volumes and volumes of articles, textbook chapters, novels. I would write seminar papers on my new computer, up there in my room, late at night, listening to music until all hours, because my schedule was under my control. That was a wonderful virtue of seminars.

When a seminar ran late into the night, draining my brain with arguments over the right interpretation of some abstract text, my friends and I would hold an informal detox session in someone's dormitory room, staying up hours more to dissect the classroom conversation. We came up with all the clever one-liners each of us should have had ready for the professor and developed all the criticisms of the readings that had eluded us earlier. Those postmortem conversations have stuck more firmly in my memory than many of the assigned readings themselves. In every campus or classroom crisis, friends were the one constant.

Alums I spoke with when I was thinking about this essay told me that the people they met in college were the lasting benefit Swarthmore provided for them. Friends were the allies in difficult classes, the sounding boards for ideas for papers and grandiose schemes to save the world—or, at least, the campus—and the folks who made sure that I did not lose myself entirely in books. The people who formed the core group I am sure to rely on for the rest of my life were the ones who weathered crises and epiphanies with me. Some courses were crises on a weekly basis. My classmates in economic theory helped me avoid spending extra months figuring out why it is that when prices decline, people consume more of what they want. Professor Saffran always tried to be kind to us, but his patience with a sloppy answer would go only so far, and then one of us would be sent to the blackboard to work out a problem alone, while everyone else watched. The resulting fear led us to set up our own study groups to rehearse. Sometimes, we succeeded in figuring out a homework problem on our own, but I remember all the times we failed. I remember having to go to the board. The epiphany was not eventually getting to the right answer; it was realizing that I was learning from the experience itself.

The crisis outside of my classes that has stayed with me resulted from the realization that not all professors knew how to teach effectively, and that I and my fellow students were paying the price. I took my concerns to faculty members I trusted; I talked them over with members of the Education Department, who knew more than I about how we learn. I finally wrote up some of my concerns and my proposed solutions and sent them to members of the College administration. We organized a meeting, and I learned how not to run a meeting. We came up with a plan, and I learned that plans require the support of the people critical to implementing them and should begin with easily managed small steps. A smaller group held a less ambitious meeting, and a few faculty members began to consider how certain classes might be taught more effectively.

It was a frustrating experience at the time, and it provoked a crisis of confidence for me. Not for months afterward, not until I was well into graduate school, did I realize that at most other schools, very few people—even friends but certainly faculty and staff—would have listened to my concerns, tolerated my memos, or considered the ideas I tried to outline in them. The surprise, in retrospect, was not that change was difficult, but that anyone was receptive to it at all. That may have been Swarthmore's last lesson, but it was not the end of the cycle of crises and epiphanies.

I work for *The New York Times*, and every day that I have to write a story presents a crisis of a sort. Hours—and sometimes days, even weeks—of reporting provide the facts that support an article, but ultimately there is, as an editor of mine at another newspaper once told me, a hole waiting in the newspaper. That hole can cause considerable stress, especially when the topic of the story becomes apparent very late in the day.

It took me years to realize that not every story would come easily, that not every opening sentence would be perfect, that not every attempt to explain a complicated subject in very little time, with very little space, would succeed. At times, writing a longer story that will not appear for days, I somehow stumble upon the exact words that I think I need to use, though I would not call that an epiphany. Perhaps searching for those words has something in common with the late-night struggle to find the best way to explain in a seminar paper the hundreds of pages of material assigned in a given week. Such college experiences certainly help me to cope with the unpredictable rhythms of the *Times.*

I need no epiphany to know that.

᠅

Jonathan Glater, a reporter for The New York Times, *currently covers law firms, consulting firms, and accounting firms.*

I Hear Voices

Sanda Balaban '94

I have a confession to make. I hear voices. Sometimes, unexpectedly, perhaps at 2 o'clock on a Tuesday afternoon, I am transported through time and space to a classroom as familiar to me as the beating of my heart. Although I can't always make out the exact words, I can distinguish the excited *thrum* that underscores the interchange of ideas. The scene is saturated with sunlight, shimmering through the room's wide windows and warming the shoulders of the students, who sit with their desks in a circle, eyes bright and mouths moist from the exertion of articulating thoughts pulled from the most passionate parts of themselves. It is as if these images are emblazoned on the inside of my eyelids; if I close my eyes, I can be whisked back to a moment seared into my subconscious more than a decade ago. Memories of Swarthmore often seem clearer to me than memories of, say, where I left my keys.

I've wondered why these recollections are so powerful. Although I certainly treasured my time at the College, I've also enjoyed the vibrancy of my postcollegiate experiences, few of which are ever evoked in the multisensory Technicolor of that particular Trotter classroom. Perhaps it's because if I hadn't experienced this kind of classroom, I never would have committed myself to trying to make other classrooms transformational sites of teaching and learning. If I hadn't benefited from the brilliant teaching of professors like Abbe Blum—whose responses to our seminar papers were often as long as the papers themselves and who was artfully able to engage with and honor our ideas while pushing us to probe deeper and develop our arguments further—I never would have aspired to become an educator myself.

Swarthmore was catalytic not only in my coming to consciousness but in determining my professional path. Although it's difficult to separate who I am from whom Swarthmore helped make me, I do know that before Swarthmore, none of the possible careers I envisioned for myself related to being a teacher or working in the field of education. The humdrummery of high school never sparked any desire to spend the rest of my life working in such a setting; yet by the time I was a junior at the College, I couldn't imagine wanting to be anywhere else. For at Swarthmore—particularly once I began to participate in seminars—I experienced the zenith of what education could be. This was an entirely different species of intellectual engagement than I had ever encountered, and I was dazzled by its possible implications for public education.

Initially, I went through a period of anger, feeling outraged that my own education at a well-regarded middle-class public high school had been so inadequate and, more disturbingly, realizing how much worse the quality of education is in most other schools across the country, particularly those (under)serving low-income children of color. Because I knew that only a privileged few would ever be able to attend Swarthmore (although thoughts of franchising Swarthmore à la Starbucks did occasionally dance like sugar plum fairies through my head), I was infused with a desire to emulate aspects of the Swarthmore experience and try to bring them to bear in K-12 classrooms. Although Swarthmore's academics

certainly prepare one to flourish in any professional field—
including those that are the most lucrative and prestigious—it
does not surprise me that such a significant proportion of its
graduates pursue "humble" careers in education.

My brother, who made the unfortunate choice to bypass
Swarthmore in favor of an Ivy League university, once chided
me for telling someone that he was hanging out with his college friends a few years after graduation. "That makes me
sound like I haven't moved on from college," he complained.
Well, perhaps *I* haven't moved on from college, for I take profound pride in maintaining relationships with respected and
beloved friends from Swarthmore and eagerly forge new
friendships with folks I didn't know during my four short
years on campus. For me, the acquisition of these friendships
alone is worth Swarthmore's sticker price. I've actively pursued interactions with alums by taking on responsibilities as
class secretary and Connection co-chair in regions where I've
lived, and I've been amazed that I almost always feel an intense
kinship with Swarthmoreans from across the years. What is it,
I've wondered, that can create such consistency in the kinds of
people who emerge from the College? Is it that the cracker-
jack staff in the Admissions Office has an uncanny ability to
identify "Swarthmore material"? Or is it that admitted students are akin to human tofu—rich in nutrients and so
absorptive of the influence of other ingredients around us that
after marinating in Swarthmore for four years, we emerge
with a distinctive flavor that transcends eras? Probably a combination of the two. There is clearly a potent culture that char-
acterizes the campus, encouraging us to open our minds and
hearts, and cultivating a kind of wide-awakeness to the world
that remains long after we graduate.

I still remember coming to the campus for the first time,
to be interviewed. I applied to the College—as well as to 15
others, many of which interested me more—at the insistent
urging of my mother (which, at the time, certainly didn't

> *I experienced the zenith of what education could be, and I was dazzled by the possible implications for public education.*

work to Swarthmore's advantage). When I agreed to visit Swarthmore, I viewed it merely as an opportunity for a "practice interview" without the high stakes of other, ostensibly more appealing, institutions. Wending my way up Magill Walk toward Parrish, I was struck by the lush beauty of the campus, but it was the beauty of what transpired after entering the building that sold me on the school. After being greeted by a woman whose name eludes me but whose kind smile I can instantly recall, we began to share ideas, impressions, and insights in an exchange that was much less an interview than it was a conversation. I realized that I wanted to continue this kind of conversation for the rest of my days. And I have done so, both literally (rarely does a week go by without some sort of stimulating discussion with an alum) and imaginatively (I conduct internal dialogues with Swarthmore professors and peers quite regularly, and these "conversations" always enrich my thinking).

Among the many things I learned at Swarthmore is the danger of essentializing, but I *have* found certain commonalities of character among Swarthmoreans: an inquisitiveness and liveliness of mind; a love of language and a desire to use it to express aspects of human experience; an appreciation of complexity; a sense of purpose and ever-unfolding possibility; a willingness to set ambitious, even audacious, goals for ourselves; a conscientiousness and creativity in questioning the realities of the world; and a commitment to taking action to improve it. Swarthmore is imbued with what I think of as intellectual activism—an appreciation of ideas not as abstractions but as applications meant to undergird ethical actions and interactions. One emerges from Swarthmore enlightened but certainly not lightened; understanding entails an obligation of sorts, and Swarthmoreans tend to carry the weight of radical responsibility in a way that many other college graduates do not. This is more of a blessing than a burden, as it enables us to achieve extraordinary things—and to be extraordinary people.

Years ago, I read a quote by Adlai Stevenson that seemed exquisitely applicable to that surreal, so-real time of our lives spent at Swarthmore:

> *Your days are short here;*
> *This is the last of your springs.*
> *And now, in the serenity and quiet of this lovely place,*
> *Touch the depths of truth, feel the hem of Heaven.*
> *You will go away with old, good friends.*
> *And don't forget, when you leave, why you came.*

I never will.

❧

Sanda Balaban recently became special assistant to the Bronx, N.Y., regional school superintendent, working on educational strategies for that borough.

A Death
in the Family

Dan Rothenberg '95

There were eight freshmen on my hall in 1991. We were a pretty close bunch that year, steadying one another as high school boyfriends and girlfriends were left behind and as Professor Phil Weinstein hurt our heads. One day, a few months in, I climbed the stairs to our third-floor dorm to find a clutch of grim-faced people standing at one end of the hall. It was Kim. Her father had died, suddenly, and she had already left campus for home. Several of us hadn't even seen her between receiving the news and departure. "How was she before she left?" Pretty bad. Terrible.

It was decided that we should go to upstate New York for the funeral. Four of us went, four 18-year-olds with sleeping bags and a set of formal clothes. The trip north has become a blur—I don't even recall if we took the train or drove. I assume we took the train.

The scene at Kim's parents' house was almost too much to take in. The adults showered us with a gratitude that frightened and embarrassed us. We did not know what to expect, but these exhalations of relief at our arrival—it was as though we had made it through a great snow with the last doses of penicillin. We embraced Kimberly one by one and waited with anxious steps for her to assure us that she was all right.

She was not all right. I had never seen someone in this state, and I did not see it again until the following year, when my grandmother died, and I watched my grandfather, a 74-year-old man with emphysema, drink bottle after bottle of vodka and weep for days on end, telling the story of how she just "went to sleep" on the sofa. So this is it, I thought. This is grief. That thing from the Shakespeare plays, it isn't for effect, it isn't poetic. It is an exact description of how it happens.

A few minutes after our arrival, Kim began to hyperventilate. She went into a kind of trance. It was as though she saw something in front of her. She became ashen, and the family friend who was "taking care of everything" said to her: "Kimberly. Kimberly. Look at me. Look at my tie. OK? Just look at my tie. Focus on my tie."

And I was struck by how this could kill a person, this grief. When they say in *King Lear* that his heart cracked, and he died—this could indeed happen. If you were frail, and you stopped breathing in your grief, if you let sobs wrack your body, the physical force of it . . . And what consolation can we offer to someone marooned in this new world, a world suddenly empty of the person who has died?

As we removed ourselves from the cloud of disaster that hung over the family, to a corner of the house, Kimberly seemed to "come out of it." She reveled in whatever gossip we could bring from the campus. When she laughed, our shoulders, which we had not known were up by our ears, came down an inch. What she wanted, what she needed, was just this—a little bit of normal. Surely we were there to be formal and respectful? No, no! . . . Once we understood, we eagerly supplied as many details—small bits of scandal, impressions of the oddities of our peers and professors—as we could. I caught glimpses of family members peeking in, drawn by her laughter, which they had not heard in days. They shot me conspir-

When they say in King Lear *that his heart cracked and he died—this could indeed happen.*

atorial glances of palpable relief; and the tearful gratitude made a little sense. She had been catatonic, they told me. They had feared for her life.

That evening, a neighbor made her entire house available for Kim and her friends from Swarthmore. With our own space, the night became the same as any slumber party, but supercharged with the desperation and relief of the falling day. The guitar came out, we lounged on one another, gave those massages that 18-year-olds allow of one another, and we howled with laughter, a laughter that was as full as any laughter I've had before or since. I caught myself at one moment about to say, "This is the most fun I've ever had." When I thought it, my face was suddenly suffused with shame. And I swore I would never tell anyone that I had forgotten myself so completely in joy, when my formal clothes for the funeral were hanging up in the next room.

The next morning, the family had left an Entenmann's ring of coffee cake for us. We devoured it, exclaiming about how delicious it was. "This is the best coffee cake I have ever had," I said, eating my third or fourth slice.

I looked for it in supermarkets in the years since then, and, once or twice, I bought the same coffee cake. But it never tasted the same, not one bit.

I make plays and performance pieces now; I still make work with people I met in college. I don't see Kim very much any more, but writing this piece put us back in touch. I needed to show her what I had written before it went into this book.

It is important to me that my descriptions of this moment, a dozen years ago, be simple and that they not try too hard to explain things that could not, in the end, be explained. Swarthmore taught me a lot about explaining, but also about the limits of explanation.

I like to think that part of what I have taken with me from Swarthmore is a spirit of humility, a belief in the virtue of *plainness*, which I imagine running beneath the College, beneath all our strivings for bravura performances.

But that's probably saying too much already.

⚬

Dan Rothenberg is co-founder and co-artistic director of the Pig Iron Theatre Company, a performance ensemble based in Philadelphia.

The "Chucky" Caper

Jason Zengerle '96

I was at Swarthmore for a good two-and-a-half years before a professor threatened to file criminal charges against me. Along with my friend and classmate Ben Seigel, I edited a campus magazine called *Spike*, which the two of us created when we were sophomores. Taking its cue from venerable professional titles like *Spy* and *Might*—OK, blatantly ripping off venerable professional titles like *Spy* and *Might*—*Spike* was our attempt to blend good writing, thorough reporting, and snarky humor into a coherent and entertaining whole. Whether we succeeded at that, it's difficult to say. One thing we undoubtedly did accomplish, however, was ticking people off. Our article on how much donors paid to get their names on campus buildings angered the Development Office; our first-person account of the sordid goings-on among Swarthmore students studying in Ireland annoyed the people who ran the Study Abroad Program; our "undercover" investigation of Strath Haven High School won us no friends in the greater Delaware County community. But it wasn't until one of our writers decided to catalog how "insecure" the Swarthmore campus was—by walking through unlocked doors and climbing through unlocked windows to gain after-hours entry to a bunch of places like the Admissions Office and labs filled with expensive equipment—that we came close to feeling the long arm of the law.

The problem was that one of the places our writer visited was the office of a professor who, perhaps not surprisingly, didn't appreciate the fact that *Spike* had told the entire campus that he did not lock his office door. And, as this professor informed Ben and me in a letter that we found in our campus mailboxes upon our return to school from winter break, he hoped to bring criminal trespassing charges against the two of us and anyone else who had been involved in the story. Of course, the professor didn't know who those others—namely, the story's writer—might be, because we had published the story, at the writer's request, under the pen name of "Chucky Des Moines." When "Chucky" originally approached *Spike*, he/she had already done all of his/her research, and Ben and I had merely told him/her to write up the results. That, Ben and I reasoned, protected us from any criminal trespassing charges; after all, we didn't do the actual trespassing, nor did we commission it. But the professor's letter made it quite clear that he would pursue *any* fruitful avenue in his determination to make sure someone paid for this transgression, which meant that there remained the not-so-small matter of what Swarthmore might do to us at the professor's behest. Would the College pull *Spike*'s funding? Would it ask Ben and me to relinquish control of the magazine? Would it ask us to take a semester off? All these possibilities occurred to us, before something else occurred to us as well: If we revealed "Chucky's" identity, would the professor focus his ire on "Chucky"—whoever he/she may be—and leave us alone?

Thus, Ben and I faced our first bona fide journalistic dilemma. It wasn't exactly the stuff of Woodward and Bernstein—"Chucky" was no Deep Throat; the professor hadn't threatened to put any of our appendages through a

> *I was at Swarthmore for a good two-and-a-half years before a professor threatened to file criminal charges against me.*

wringer—but it was a dilemma nonetheless. Although I take no pride in the fact that I, at least, did briefly flirt with the idea of selling out "Chucky" to save our hides, I'm relieved that I can look back and say that we ultimately decided that revealing the writer's real name was out of the question. Still, that didn't mean we didn't think the College might try to force us into making such a revelation, and as we headed into our meeting with the dean on whose desk this little matter had landed, we promised each other that, no matter what the dean threatened us with, we would take "Chucky's" identity with us to the grave.

Those melodramatic promises, it turned out, were completely unnecessary. First, the dean did not try to force Ben and me to reveal "Chucky's" identity. What's more, he told us that we were welcome to continue our studies at Swarthmore, that we could stay on as editors of the magazine we had founded, and that the College would even continue to pay for *Spike's* publication. But with Swarthmore's sword of Damocles sheathed, the dean didn't completely let us off the hook. What, he wanted to know, had we hoped to accomplish by running such a story? We told him that we had intended to point out how easily Swarthmore's community of trust could be exploited, much in the way a television news reporter sneaks into the local nuclear power plant to blow the whistle on how insecure the facility is. But why, the dean asked, hadn't we just approached the College before we published the article to see if it had any good answers to our concerns and then, if we weren't satisfied with the answers, run the story? It was a good question and one that forced us to admit that, although we did have some high-minded reasons for running it, we also had some not-so-high-minded ones as well: Just as the television-news reporter inevitably runs his nuclear-power plant story during ratings-sweeps weeks, we thought the campus-security article was a good read.

Now, was that good read ultimately worth letting the whole campus know how easy it was to get into some places people probably shouldn't be able to get into? That was an open question, but it wasn't one that we had honestly wrestled with until the dean made us do so. I don't think we ever did answer it that day, but, after promising that we would keep the question in mind when we decided on future articles, we left the Dean's Office and went on to edit *Spike* for another year-and-a-half without serious incident. (Yes, without serious incident; by the time *Spike* decided to comb through faculty members' garbage cans and report on the contents, Ben and I had already graduated.)

The point of this shaggy dog story? That, whatever other meanings Swarthmore may have, the most important one to me is that it is the kind of place where young people are given the room to make mistakes and then to learn from them. I'm not saying that Swarthmore was so permissive that all mistakes were tolerated. They weren't. But, more often than not, in instances where there were gray areas, or where there was no malicious intent, the College admirably refrained from lowering the boom. The thinking seemed to be: Punishment didn't necessarily facilitate learning.

And I did learn. In my career so far as a professional journalist, I've been involved in a handful of situations that have raised questions similar to the ones I encountered in the Chucky Des Moines affair, and I like to think that I handled those questions more forthrightly, and answered them more intelligently, because of what I experienced at Swarthmore. But, more important, I can think of other lessons—lessons less suitable for publication in this book because they are either more personal or less entertaining than those learned as the editor of a campus magazine—that have helped me in my development, not as a journalist but as a person. I left Swarthmore a different person from who I was when I arrived there. And, today, I think that I am a different person from who I was when I left Swarthmore seven years ago because, I believe, I am still processing some of the lessons I learned there.

◈◈

Jason Zengerle, an associate editor at The New Republic, *also writes for other publications.*